PIANO

100 YEARS OF
BROADWAY
A CENTENNIAL COLLECTION OF SONG

WITHDRAWN

CONTRA COSTA COUNTY LIBRARY

This publication is not for sale in
the EC and/or Australia
or New Zealand.

ISBN 0-7935-2964-6

HAL•LEONARD™
CORPORATION

7777 W. BLUEMOUND RD. P.O. BOX 13819 MILWAUKEE, WI 53213

Copyright © 1994 by HAL LEONARD CORPORATION
International Copyright Secured   All Rights Reserved

For all works contained herein:
Unauthorized copying, arranging, adapting, recording or public performance is an infringement of copyright.
Infringers are liable under the law.

3 1901 02107 2865

Chronological Listing

YEAR	SONG TITLE/SHOW	PAGE
1893	After the Ball from A TRIP TO CHINATOWN	36
1896	You're a Grand Old Flag from GEORGE WASHINGTON, JR.	40
1898	Gypsy Love Song from THE FORTUNE TELLER	44
1900	Tell Me Pretty Maiden from FLORODORA	47
1903	Toyland from BABES IN TOYLAND	53
1904	Give My Regards to Broadway from LITTLE JOHNNY JONES	56
1905	How'd You Like to Spoon With Me from THE EARL AND THE GIRL	60
1907	Vilia from THE MERRY WIDOW	64
1910	Italian Street Song from NAUGHTY MARIETTA	70
1911	Woodman, Woodman, Spare That Tree! from ZIEGFELD FOLLIES OF 1911	74
1912	Giannina Mia from THE FIREFLY	78
1914	They Didn't Believe Me from THE GIRL FROM UTAH	82
1915	I Love a Piano from STOP! LOOK! LISTEN!	86
1917	Till the Clouds Roll By from OH BOY!	91
1918	Rock-a-Bye Your Baby With a Dixie Melody from SINBAD	96
1919	A Pretty Girl Is Like a Melody from ZIEGFELD FOLLIES	100
1920	Look For the Silver Lining from SALLY	104
1921	Everybody Step from MUSIC BOX REVUE	108
1922	I'll Build a Stairway to Paradise from GEORGE WHITE'S SCANDALS	113
1924	Indian Love Call from ROSE-MARIE	117
1925	Manhattan from GARRICK GAIETIES	121
1926	Someone to Watch Over Me from OH, KAY!	125
1927	Ol' Man River from SHOW BOAT	129
1928	I Can't Give You Anything But Love from BLACKBIRDS OF 1928	134
1929	Why Was I Born? from SWEET ADELINE	137
1930	Love For Sale from THE NEW YORKERS	141
1931	Who Cares? (So Long As You Care For Me) from OF THEE I SING	145
1932	The Song Is You from MUSIC IN THE AIR	149
1933	Supper Time from AS THOUSANDS CHEER	153
1934	You're the Top from ANYTHING GOES	157
1935	My Romance from JUMBO	160
1936	There's a Small Hotel from ON YOUR TOES	163
1937	Where or When from BABES IN ARMS	166
1938	September Song from KNICKERBOCKER HOLIDAY	169
1939	Well, Did You Evah? from DUBARRY WAS A LADY	173
1940	Bewitched from PAL JOEY	178
1941	The Saga of Jenny from LADY IN THE DARK	182
1942	Nobody's Heart from BY JUPITER	188
1943	Oh, What a Beautiful Mornin' from OKLAHOMA!	190
1944	Lonely Town from ON THE TOWN	192
1945	If I Loved You from CAROUSEL	198
1946	I Got the Sun in the Morning from ANNIE GET YOUR GUN	200
1947	How Are Things in Glocca Morra from FINIAN'S RAINBOW	205
1948	Brush Up Your Shakespeare from KISS ME, KATE	208

Standing on a corner   MOST HAPPY FELLA ?

1949	Some Enchanted Evening from SOUTH PACIFIC	213
1950	Luck Be a Lady from GUYS AND DOLLS	216
1951	Hello, Young Lovers from THE KING AND I	221
1952	Wish You Were Here from WISH YOU WERE HERE	224
1953	Stranger in Paradise from KISMET	226
1954	A Sleepin' Bee from HOUSE OF FLOWERS	229
1955	All of You from SILK STOCKINGS	233
1956	I've Grown Accustomed to Her Face from MY FAIR LADY	237
1957	Till There Was You from THE MUSIC MAN	239
1958	You Are Beautiful from FLOWER DRUM SONG	241
1959	Everything's Coming Up Roses from GYPSY	243
1960	Camelot from CAMELOT	248
1961	I Believe in You from HOW TO SUCCEED IN BUSINESS WITHOUT REALLY TRYING	254
1962	Comedy Tonight from A FUNNY THING HAPPENED ON THE WAY TO THE FORUM	257
1963	Where Is Love? from OLIVER!	260
1964	Hello, Dolly! from HELLO, DOLLY!	262
1965	The Impossible Dream (The Quest) from MAN OF LA MANCHA	265
1966	Cabaret from CABARET	269
1967	Maman from MATA HARI	272
1968	Promises, Promises from PROMISES, PROMISES	275
1969	Somebody from CELEBRATION	280
1970	Being Alive from COMPANY	285
1971	Broadway Baby from FOLLIES	288
1972	Summer Nights from GREASE	291
1973	Send in the Clowns from A LITTLE NIGHT MUSIC	295
1974	I Won't Send Roses from MACK AND MABEL	298
1975	What I Did for Love from A CHORUS LINE	301
1976	Pretty Lady from PACIFIC OVERTURES	305
1977	It's the Hard-Knock Life from ANNIE	313
(1938) 1978	The Joint Is Jumpin' from AIN'T MISBEHAVIN'	317
1979	Don't Cry for Me Argentina from EVITA	(321)
(1935) 1980	Lullaby of Broadway from 42ND STREET	327
1981	And I Am Telling You I'm Not Going from DREAMGIRLS	330
1982	Memory from CATS	(339)
1983	The Best of Times from LA CAGE AUX FOLLES	343
1984	Sunday from SUNDAY IN THE PARK WITH GEORGE	350
1985	Unexpected Song from SONG & DANCE	355
1986	Leaning on a Lamp-Post from ME AND MY GIRL	360
1987	Bring Him Home from LES MISÉRABLES	(364)
1988	The Music of the Night from THE PHANTOM OF THE OPERA	(368)
1989	Bonjour Amour from GRAND HOTEL	373
1990	Love Changes Everything from ASPECTS OF LOVE	381
1991	Sun and Moon from MISS SAIGON	385
1992	Embraceable You from CRAZY FOR YOU	390
1993	The Kiss of the Spider Woman from KISS OF THE SPIDER WOMAN	394

Alphabetical Listing

36	After the Ball from A TRIP TO CHINATOWN *1893*
233	All of You from SILK STOCKINGS *1955*
330	And I Am Telling You I'm Not Going from DREAMGIRLS *1981*
285	Being Alive from COMPANY *1970*
343	The Best of Times from LA CAGE AUX FOLLES *1983*
178	Bewitched from PAL JOEY *1940*
373	Bonjour Amour from GRAND HOTEL *1989*
364	Bring Him Home from LES MISÉRABLES *1987*
288	Broadway Baby from FOLLIES *1971*
208	Brush Up Your Shakespeare from KISS ME, KATE *1948*
269	Cabaret from CABARET *1966*
248	Camelot from CAMELOT *1960*
257	Comedy Tonight from A FUNNY THING HAPPENED ON THE WAY TO THE FORUM *1962*
321	Don't Cry For Me Argentina from EVITA *1979*
390	Embraceable You from CRAZY FOR YOU *1992*
108	Everybody Step from MUSIC BOX REVUE *1921*
243	Everything's Coming Up Roses from GYPSY *1959*
78	Giannina Mia from THE FIREFLY *1912*
56	Give My Regards to Broadway from LITTLE JOHNNY JONES *1904*
44	Gypsy Love Song from THE FORTUNE TELLER *1898*
262	Hello, Dolly! from HELLO, DOLLY! *1964*
221	Hello, Young Lovers from THE KING AND I *1951*
205	How Are Things in Glocca Morra from FINIAN'S RAINBOW *1947*
60	How'd You Like to Spoon With Me from THE EARL AND THE GIRL *1905*
254	I Believe in You from HOW TO SUCCEED IN BUSINESS WITHOUT REALLY TRYING *1961*
134	I Can't Give You Anything But Love from BLACKBIRDS OF 1928 *1928*
200	I Got the Sun in the Morning from ANNIE GET YOUR GUN *1946*
86	I Love a Piano from STOP! LOOK! LISTEN! *1915*
298	I Won't Send Roses from MACK AND MABEL *1974*
113	I'll Build a Stairway to Paradise from GEORGE WHITE'S SCANDALS *1922*
237	I've Grown Accustomed to Her Face from MY FAIR LADY *1956*
198	If I Loved You from CAROUSEL *1945*
265	The Impossible Dream (The Quest) from MAN OF LA MANCHA *1965*
117	Indian Love Call from ROSE-MARIE *1924*
313	It's the Hard-Knock Life from ANNIE *1977*
70	Italian Street Song from NAUGHTY MARIETTA *1910*
317	The Joint Is Jumpin' from AIN'T MISBEHAVIN' *1978*
394	The Kiss of the Spider Woman from KISS OF THE SPIDER WOMAN *1993*
360	Leaning on a Lamp-Post from ME AND MY GIRL *1986*
192	Lonely Town from ON THE TOWN *1944*
104	Look For the Silver Lining from SALLY *1920*
381	Love Changes Everything from ASPECTS OF LOVE *1990*
141	Love For Sale from THE NEW YORKERS *1930*
216	Luck Be a Lady from GUYS AND DOLLS *1950*
327	Lullaby of Broadway from 42ND STREET *1980*
272	Maman from MATA HARI *1967*
121	Manhattan from GARRICK GAIETIES *1925*
339	Memory from CATS *1982*
368	The Music of the Night from THE PHANTOM OF THE OPERA *1988*
160	My Romance from JUMBO *1935*
188	Nobody's Heart from BY JUPITER *1942*
190	Oh, What A Beautiful Mornin' from OKLAHOMA! *1943*
129	Ol' Man River from SHOW BOAT *1927*
100	A Pretty Girl Is Like a Melody from ZIEGFELD FOLLIES *1919*
305	Pretty Lady from PACIFIC OVERTURES *1976*
275	Promises, Promises from PROMISES, PROMISES *1968*
96	Rock-a-Bye Your Baby With a Dixie Melody from SINBAD *1918*
182	The Saga of Jenny from LADY IN THE DARK *1941*
295	Send in the Clowns from A LITTLE NIGHT MUSIC *1973*
169	September Song from KNICKERBOCKER HOLIDAY *1938*
229	A Sleepin' Bee from HOUSE OF FLOWERS *1954*
280	Somebody from CELEBRATION *1969*
213	Some Enchanted Evening from SOUTH PACIFIC *1949*
125	Someone to Watch Over Me from OH, KAY! *1926*
149	The Song Is You from MUSIC IN THE AIR *1932*
226	Stranger in Paradise from KISMET *1953*
291	Summer Nights from GREASE *1972*
385	Sun and Moon from MISS SAIGON *1991*
350	Sunday from SUNDAY IN THE PARK WITH GEORGE *1984*
153	Supper Time from AS THOUSANDS CHEER *1933*
47	Tell Me Pretty Maiden from FLORODORA *1900*
163	There's a Small Hotel from ON YOUR TOES *1936*
82	They Didn't Believe Me from THE GIRL FROM UTAH *1914*
91	Till the Clouds Roll By from OH BOY! *1917*
239	Till There Was You from THE MUSIC MAN *1957*
53	Toyland from BABES IN TOYLAND *1903*
355	Unexpected Song from SONG & DANCE *1985*
64	Vilia from THE MERRY WIDOW *1907*
173	Well, Did You Evah? from DUBARRY WAS A LADY *1939*
301	What I Did For Love from A CHORUS LINE *1975*
260	Where Is Love? from OLIVER! *1963*
166	Where or When from BABES IN ARMS *1937*
145	Who Cares? (So Long As You Care For Me) from OF THEE I SING *1931*
137	Why Was I Born? from SWEET ADELINE *1929*
224	Wish You Were Here from WISH YOU WERE HERE *1952*
74	Woodman, Woodman, Spare That Tree! from ZIEGFELD FOLLIES OF 1911 *1911*
241	You Are Beautiful from FLOWER DRUM SONG *1958*
40	You're a Grand Old Flag from GEORGE WASHINGTON, JR. *1896*
157	You're the Top from ANYTHING GOES *1934*

The Broadway Tradition —
100 Years in Times Square

Prior to 1893 New York theatrical life took place exclusively downtown, that is, south of 40th Street — way south in most cases. The city bustled in lower Manhattan, but anything north of about 36th Street was considered practically rural. With the building of the American Theater at 42nd Street and 8th Avenue the great change began, moving the town's heartbeat uptown by a couple of neighborhoods. 42nd Street in 1893 was a residential area, with a few general stores and churches spelling the rows of apartments and houses. Theater manager T. Henry Smith, partner and son of publisher Samuel French, saw this area of the city as ripe for investment. With a capacity of 2100 (plus 200 standees), the American Theater was a large, stylish home for melodramas and other entertainments. The building was completely wired for electricity, certainly bringing in some visitors just to see what was then still quite rare. A gold dome, 57 feet in diameter, was the auditorium's ceiling. The house was decorated with elaborately painted murals, and gargoyles looked down on those in attendance from the side walls. The theater boasted a roof garden, open before and after the show, and even contained one of the first elevators in New York.

With the American leading the way, within a few years "The Great White Way" had been defined, and theaters had sprung up all around the Times Square area. This theatrical district — our most accomplished and important national theatrical presence — has rarely been stable. The theatres have changed (the American is long gone), the styles of the music have changed many times, the plays have changed so often that it is almost impossible to piece together an accurate history of performances. The country has changed so thoroughly that virtually nothing about the America of 1893 is still familiar to us. But the Broadway tradition, seeded in that year, has survived, thrived and flourished. When the history of the 20th century is written, what we know as Broadway will stand as the centerpiece of truly American art expressive of its time.

Here is a highly selective, almost arbitrary (except by chronology) "walking tour" through the song history of the Broadway theater tradition. Step lively along the way, and

Come on along and listen to the lullaby of Broadway...

The Shows and Songs
A year by year guide to the major musicals to play on Broadway, 1893-1993.

1893   *Featured Song Selection:*
After the Ball (interpolated)
from *A Trip to Chinatown*

Notable Musical Openings of the Year:

ROBIN HOOD
music by Reginald de Koven, lyrics by Harry B. Smith opened in 1993 for one of several New York appearances
selected songs: All Is Fair in Love and War; Auctioneer's Song; The Bells of Saint Swithins; Come the Bowmen in Lincoln Green; Happy Day! Happy Day!; I Come as a Cavalier; Tinker's Song; 'Neath the Greenwood Tree; 'Tis the Morning of the Fair; Though It Was Within This Hour We Met
cast: The Boston Ideal Company

A TRIP TO CHINATOWN
music by Percy Gaunt with interpolated numbers, lyrics & book by Charles Hoyt
opened on Broadway 11/9/93 for a run of 657 performances
selected songs: After the Ball; The Bowery; Push the Clouds Away; Reuben, Reuben (sometimes known as Ruben and Cynthia)
cast: J. Aldrich Libby, Harry Conor; Loie Fuller

1894   *Notable Musical Openings of the Year:*

THE PASSING SHOW (An Extravaganza)
music by Ludwig Englander, book & lyrics by Sydney Rosenberg
opened on Broadway 5/12/94
cast: Jefferson de Angelis, Adele Ritchie, Johnny Henshaw, Paul Arthur

ROB ROY
music by Reginald de Koven, book & lyrics by Harry B. Smith
opened on Broadway 10/29/94 for a run of 168 performances
selected songs: Come, Lads of the Highlands; Dearest of My Heart; Lay of the Cavalier; My Home Is Where the Heather Blooms
cast: William Pruette, Lizzie Machnicol, Juliette Cordon, Joseph Herbert

PRINCE ANANIAS
music by Victor Herbert, lyrics & book by Francis Neilson
opened on Broadway 11/20/94
selected songs: Ah! Cupid, Meddlesome Boy!; Ah! List to Me; Amaryllis; I Am No Queen; It Needs No Poet!
cast: Mena McCleary, W. H. MacDonald, Eugene Cowles, Henry Clay Barnabee, George Frothingham, Jessie Bartlett Davis, Josephine Bartlett

1895   *Notable Musical Openings of the Year:*

PRINCESS BONNIE
music, lyrics & book by Willard Spencer
opened, on Broadway 9/2/95 for a run of 40 performances
cast: Fred Lennox Jr., William M. Arnstrong, George O'Donnell, Hilda Clark

THE WIZARD OF THE NILE
music by Victor Herbert, book & lyrics by Harry B. Smith
opened on Broadway 11/4/95 for a run of 105 performances
selected songs: My Angeline; Pure and White is the Lotus; Star Light, Star Bright; Stonecutter's Song
cast: Frank Daniels, Walter Allen, Edwin Isham, Dorothy Morton, Helen Redmond

1896   *Notable Musical Openings of the Year:*

EL CAPITAN
music by John Philip Sousa, lyrics by Thomas Frost, book by Charles Klein
opened on Broadway 4/20/96 for the first of several New York appearances
selected songs: Behold El Capitan; If You Examine Human Kind; O, Spare a Daughter's Aching Heart; Semper Fidelis; A Typical Tune of Zanzibar; When We Hear the Call for Battle; You See in Me, My Friends
cast: De Wolf Hopper, Edna Wallace Hopper, Alice Hosmer, Bertha Waltzinger, Edmund Stanley, Charles Klein

THE ART OF MARYLAND (A Weber and Fields Extravaganza)
music by John Stromberg, lyrics & book by Joseph Herbert
opened on Broadway 9/5/96
cast: Weber and Fields, Lottie Gilson, Sam Bernard, John T. Kelly, The Beaumont Sisters

THE GOLD BUG
music by Victor Herbert, lyrics & book by Glen MacDonough
opened on Broadway 9/21/96 selected songs: Gold Bug March; One For Another; The Owl and the Thrush
cast: Marie Cahill, Max Figman, Molly Fuller, Bert Williams & George Walker

1897   *Notable Musical Openings of the Year:*

THE SERENADE
music by Victor Herbert, lyrics & book by Harry B. Smith
opened on Broadway 3/16/97 for a run of 79 performances
selected songs: Cupid and I; I Love Thee, I Adore Thee; The Monk and the Maid; With Cracking of Whip and Rattle of Spur
cast: Eugene Cowles, Jessie Bartlett Davis, Henry Clay Barnabee, Alice Nielsen

THE BELLE OF NEW YORK
music by Gustave Kerker, book & lyrics by Hugh Morton
opened on Broadway 9/28/97 for a run of 56 performances
selected songs: She Is the Belle of New York; Teach Me How To Kiss; They All Follow Me
cast: Edna May, Harry Davenport

THE IDOL'S EYE
music by Victor Herbert, lyrics & book by Harry B. Smith
opened on Broadway 10/25/97 for a run of seven weeks
selected songs: Cuban Song; I'm Captain Cholly Chumley of the Guards; The Lady and the Kick; Song of the Priestess
cast: Frank Daniels, Helen Redmond, Maurice Darcy, Alf C. Whelan, Will Danforth

THE HIGHWAYMAN
music by Reginald de Koven, lyrics & book by Harry B. Smith
opened on Broadway 12/13/97 for a run of 144 performances
selected songs: Do You Remember, Love?; Gypsy Sing; Highwayman Song; Moonlight Song
cast: Jerome Sykes, Joseph O'Mara, Hilda Clark

1898   *Featured Song Selection:*
Gypsy Love Song
from *The Fortune Teller*

Notable Musical Openings of the Year:

THE FORTUNE TELLER
music by Victor Herbert, lyrics & book by Harry B. Smith
opened on Broadway 9/26/98 for a run of 40 performances
selected songs: Always Do as People Say You Should; Czardas; Gypsy Love Song; Only in the Play; Romany Life
cast: Alice Nielsen, Eugene Cowles, Frank Rushworth, Marguerite Silva, Joseph Herbert, Joseph Cawthorn, May Boley

HURLY BURLY (A Weber and Fields Extravaganza)
music by John Stromberg, lyrics & book by Edgar & Harry B. Smith
opened on Broadway 9/8/98
cast: Weber and Fields, Fay Templeton

1899   *Notable Musical Openings of the Year:*

CYRANO DE BERGERAC
music by Victor Herbert, lyrics by Harry B. Smith, book by Stuart Reed
opened on Broadway 9/18/99 for a run of 28 performances
selected songs: Cadets of Gascony; I Wonder; Let the Sun of My Eyes; Since I Am Not For Thee
cast: Francis Wilson, Lulu Glaser, Josephine Intropidi, Charles H. Bowers

THE ROGERS BROTHERS IN WALL STREET (A Vaudeville Farce)
music by Maurice Levi, lyrics by J. Cheever Goodwin, book by John J. McNally opened on Broadway 9/18/99 for a run of 108 performances
Selected songs; The Belle of Murray Hill
cast: Max & Gus Rogers, Ada Lewis, Georgia Caine

WHIRL-I-GIG (A Weber and Fields Extravaganza)
music by John Stromberg, lyrics by Harry B. Smith, book by Edgar Smith
opened on Broadway 9/21/99 for a run of 264 performances
cast: Weber & Fields, Peter F. Dailey, David Warfield, Lillian Russell

1900   *Featured Song Selection:*
Tell Me, Pretty Maiden Gypsy
from *Floradora*

Notable Musical Openings of the Year:

THE CASINO GIRL
music by Ludwig Englander & John M. Flynn, lyrics & book by Harry B. Smith & John M. Flynn
opened on Broadway 3/19/00 for a run of 91 performances
selected songs: Mam'selle; New York; Slave Dealer's Song; Sweet Annie Moore
cast: Virginia Earle, Albert Hart, Sam Bernard, Mabelle Gilman, Lotta Faust

FIDDLE-DE-DEE (A Weber and Fields Extravaganza)
music by John Stromberg, lyrics by Harry B. Smith, book by Edgar Smith
opened on Broadway 9/21/00 for a run of 262 performances
cast: De Wolf Hopper, David Warfield, Fay Templeton, Lillian Russell

THE BELLE OF BOHEMIA
music by Ludwig Englander & T. MacConnell, lyrics & book by
Harry B. Smith
opened on Broadway 9/24/00 for a run of 55 performances
selected songs: He Was a Married Man; Plain Kelly McGuire;
When Shall I Find Him?
cast: Sam Bernard, Irene Bentley, Virginia Earle, Trixie Friganza

FLORODORA
music by Leslie Stuart, lyrics by Leslie Stuart, Paul Rubens & Frank
Clement, book by Owen Hall
opened on Broadway 11/12/00 for a run of 553 performances
selected songs: I Want to Be A Military Man; The Shade of the Palm; Tell
Me, Pretty Maiden; When I Leave Town
cast: Edna Wallace Hopper, Fannie Johnston, Willie Edouin, Sydney Deane,
R. E. Graham, May Edouin

Notable Musical Openings of the Year:

KING DODO
music by Gustav Luders, lyrics & book by Frank Pixley
opened on Broadway 5/12/02 for a run of 64 performances
selected songs: Diana; The Lad Who Leads; The Tale of a Bumble Bee
cast: Raymond Hitchcock, Margaret McKinney, Greta Riley,
Gertrude Quinlan

A CHINESE HONEYMOON
music by Gustave Kerker & Howard Talbot, lyrics & book by George Dance
opened on Broadway 6/2/02 for a run of 376 performances
selected songs: À la Girl; I Want to Be a Loidy; Mister Dooley;
Twiddley Bits
cast: Thomas Q. Seabrooke, Adele Ritchie, William Pruette,
Annie Yeamans

TWIRLY WHIRLY (A Weber and Fields Extravaganza)
music by Joseph Stromberg, lyrics by Edgar & Harry B. Smith,
book by Edgar Smith
opened on Broadway 9/11/02 for a run of 244 performances
cast: Weber and Fields, William Collier, Peter F. Cailey,
Lillian Russell, Mabel Barrison, Bessie Clayton

1903 *Featured Song Selection:*
Toyland
from *Babes In Toyland*

Notable Musical Openings of the Year:

THE WIZARD OF OZ
music by Paul Tietjens & A. Baldwin Sloane, lyrics & book by
L. Frank Baum
opened on Broadway 1/20/03 for a run of 293 performances
selected songs: Alas for a Man Without Brains; Hurrah for
Baffin's Bay; Sammy; When You Love Love Love
cast: David Montgomery, Fred Stone, Anna Laughlin,
Arthur Hill, Bessie Wynn, Grace Kimball

THE PRINCE OF PILSEN
music by Gustave Luders, lyrics by Frank Pixley
opened on Broadway 3/17/03
selected songs: He Didn't Know Exactly What to Do;
Heidelberg; The Message of the Violet; The Modern Pirate; To
Fun and Folly; The Tale of the Sea Shell; We Know It's Wrong
for Girls to Flirt; We'll Have a Gala Day; We've Had a Stormy
Trip; When You Are Mine
cast: Donaldson, Ransome, Helen Bertram, Anna Lichter,
Albert Parr, Lillian Coleman

THE RUNAWAYS (An Extravaganza)
music by Raymond Hubbell, lyrics & book by
Addison Burkhardt
opened on Broadway 5/11/03 for a run of 167 performances
selected songs: If I Were a Bright Little Star; A Kiss For Each
Day of the Week
cast: Alexander Clark, Edna Goodright, Dorothy Dorr,
Arthur Dunn, William Gould

WHOOP-DE-DOO (A Weber and Fields Extravaganza)
music by W. T. Francis, lyrics & book by Edgar Smith
opened on Broadway 9/24/03 for a run of 151 performances
cast: Weber and Fields, Peter F. Dailey, Louis Mann,
Carter De Haven, Lillian Russell

BABES IN TOYLAND
music by Victor Herbert, lyrics & book by Glen MacDonough
opened on Broadway 10/13/03 for a run of 192 performances
selected songs: Go to Sleep; I Can't Do the Sum; March of the
Toys; Never Mind, Bo-Peep; Song of the Poet; Toyland
cast: William Norris, Mabel Barrison, George Denham,
Bessie Wynn

Featured Song Selection:
Give My Regards to Broadway
from *Little Johnny Jones*

Notable Musical Openings of the Year:

PIFF, PAFF, POUF
music by Jean Schwartz, lyrics by William Jerome, book by
Stanislaus Stange
opened on Broadway 4/2/04 for a run of 264 performances
selected songs: The Ghost That Never Walked; Good Night, My Own
True Love; Love, Love, Love; The Radium Dance
cast: Joseph Miron, Alice Fischer, Eddie Foy, Mabel Hollins

THE SHO-GUN
music by Gustav Luders, lyrics by George Ade
opened on Broadway 10/10/04 for a run of 125 performances
selected songs: Flutter Little Bird; I Am Truly Yours; I'll Live for You;
Little Moozoo May
cast: Edward Martindel, Georgia Caine, Charles Evans

Notable Musical Openings of the Year:

HOITY TOITY (A Weber and Fields Extravaganza)
music by John Stromberg, lyrics by Harry B. Smith, book by Edgar Smith
opened on Broadway 9/15/01 for a run of 225 performances
cast: De Wolf Hopper, Sam Bernard, Lillian Russell, Fay Templeton,
Bessie Clayton

THE STROLLERS
music by Ludwig Englander, lyrics & book by Harry B. Smith, based on
Die Landesstreicher, by L. Kremm and C. Lindau
opened on Broadway 6/24/01 for a run of 70 performances
selected songs: The Ballet of the Fans; Gossip Chorus; A Lesson in
Flirtation; Strollers We
cast: Ilse Marvenga, Howard Marsh, George Hassell, Greek Evans

MR. WIX OF WICKHAM
music by Herbert Darnley, George Everhard & Jerome Kern, lyrics & book
by Herbert Darnley & John H. Wagner
opened on Broadway 9/19/04 for a run of 41 performances
selected songs: Angling by the Babbling Brook; From Saturday 'Til
Monday; Susan; Waiting for You
cast: Frank Lalor, Thelma Fair, Harry C. Clarke, Julian Eltinge

HIGGELDY PIGGELDY (A Weber and Fields Extravaganza)
music by Maurice Levi, lyrics & book by Edgar Smith
opened on Broadway 10/20/04 for a run of 185 performances
cast: Joseph Weber, Anna Held, Marie Dressler

LITTLE JOHNNY JONES
music, lyrics & book by George M. Cohan
opened on Broadway 11/7/04 for a run of 52 performances
selected songs: Give My Regards to Broadway; Life's a Funny Proposition
After All; The Yankee Doodle Boy
cast: George M. Cohan, Jerry Cohan, Helen Cohan, Donald Brian,
Ethel Levey, Tom Lewis

IT HAPPENED IN NORDLAND
music by Victor Herbert, lyrics & book by Glen McDonough
opened on Broadway 12/5/04 for a run of 154 performances
selected songs: Absinth Frappé; Al Fresco; Commandress-in-Chief;
The Knot of Blue; The Woman in the Case
cast: Lew Fields, Harry Davenport, Bessie Clayton, Joseph Herbert,
Marie Cahill

1905   *Featured Song Selection:*
How'd You Like to Spoon With Me?
from *The Earl and the Girl*

Notable Musical Openings of the Year:

FANTANA
music by Raymond Hubbell, lyrics by Robert B. Smith, book by
Sam S. Schubert & Robert B. Smith
opened on Broadway 1/14/05 for a run of 298 performances
selected songs: The Farewell Waltz; My Word; That's Art; What Would
Mrs. Grundy Say?
cast: Jefferson de Angelis, Adele Ritchie, Katie Barry, Julia Sanderson,
Douglas Fairbanks Sr.

THE EARL AND THE GIRL
music and lyrics by various writers, including Jerome Kern and Ivan Caryll
opened on Broadway 11/4/05 for a run of 148 performances
selected songs: How'd You Like to Spoon with Me
cast: Georgia Caine

A SOCIETY CIRCUS (A Hippodrome Extravaganza)
music by Manuel Klein & Gustav Luders, lyrics by Sydney Rosebfeld &
Manuel Klein, book by Sydney Rosenfeld
opened on Broadway 12/13/05 for a run of 596 performances

MLLE. MODISTE
music by Victor Herbert, lyrics & book by Henry Blossom
opened on Broadway 12/25/05 for a run of 202 performances
selected songs: I Want What I Want When I Want It; Kiss Me Again;
The Mascot of the Troop; The Time, the Place and the Girl
cast: Fritzi Scheff, Walter Percival, William Pruette, Claude Gillingwater,
Josephine Bartlett

1906   *Featured Song Selection:*
You're a Grand Old Flag
from *George Washington Jr.*

Notable Musical Openings of the Year:

FORTY-FIVE MINUTES FROM BROADWAY
Music, lyrics & book by George M. Cohan
opened on Broadway 1/1/06 for a run of 90 performances
selected songs: I Want to Be a Popular Millionaire; Mary's a Grand Old
Name; So Long Mary; Forty-five Minutes From Broadway
cast: Fay Templeton, Victor Moore, Donald Brian, Lois Ewell

TWIDDLE TWADDLE (A Weber and Fields Extravaganza)
music by Maurice Levy, lyrics & book by Edgar Smith
opened on Broadway 1/1/06 for a run of 137 performances
cast: Joe Weber, Marie Dressler, Trixie Friganza

GEORGE WASHINGTON, JR.
music, lyrics & book by George M. Cohan
opened on Broadway 2/12/06 for a run of 81 performances
selected songs: All Aboard for Broadway; I Was Born in Virginia; You're a
Grand Old Flag
cast: The Four Cohans, Ethel Levey

THE RED MILL
music by Victor Herbert, lyrics & book by Henry Blossom
opened on Broadway 9/24/06 for a run of 274 performances
selected songs: Because You're You; The Isle of Our Dreams; Every Day Is
Ladies Day With Me; Moonbeams; The Streets of New York; When You're
Pretty and the World is Fair
cast: David Montgomery, Fred Stone, Augusta Greenleaf, Joseph Ratliff,
Allene Crater, Edward Begley

THE RICH MR. HOGGENHEIMER
music by Ludwig Englander, lyrics & book by Harry B. Smith
opened on Broadway 10/22/06 for a run of 187 performances
selected songs: Any Old Time at All; Don't You Want a Paper Dearie?;
This World Is a Toy Shop
cast: Sam Bernard, Marion Garson, Georgia Caine

A PARISIAN MODEL
music by Max Hoffmann with additional songs by Will D. Cobb & Gus
Edwards, lyrics & book by Harry B. Smith
opened on Broadway 11/27/06 for a run of 179 performances
selected songs: A Gown for Each Hour of the Day; I Just Can't Make My
Eyes Behave; I'd Like to See a Little More of You
cast: Anna Held, Henry Leoni, Truly Shattuck

PIONEER DAYS (A Hippodrome Extravaganza)
music & lyrics by Manuel Klein, book by Caroll Fleming
opened on Broadway 11/28/06 for a run of 288 performances

1907   *Featured Song Selection:*
Vilia
from *The Merry Widow*

Notable Musical Openings of the Year:

THE ZIEGFELD FOLLIES OF 1907
music & lyrics by various writers, sketches by Harry B. Smith
opened on Broadway 7/8/07 for a run of 70 performances
selected songs: Budweiser's a Friend of Mine; I Think I Oughtn't Auto any
More; Handle Me With Care; Miss Ginger from Jamaica; Bye Bye, Dear
Old Broadway
cast: Grace LaRue, Mlle. Dazie, Prince Tokio, Emma Carus,
Harry Watson Jr., Marion Sunshine & Florence Tempest, George Bickel,
Helen Broderick, Nora Bayes (added)

THE AUTO RACE (A Hippodrome Extravaganza)
music by Manuel Klein, lyrics & book by Manuel Klein &
Edward P. Temple
opened on Broadway 12/25/07 for a run of 312 performances

HIP! HIP! HOORAY (A Weber and Fields Extravaganza)
music by Gus Edwards, lyrics & book by Edgar Smith
opened on Broadway 10/10/07 for a run of 64 performances
cast: Joe Weber, Velaska Suratt, Bessie Clayton

THE MERRY WIDOW
music by Franz Lehar, lyrics by Adrian Ross, book by Basil Hood
(uncredited)
opened on Broadway 10/21/07 for a run of 416 performances
selected songs: A Dutiful Wife; The Girls at Maxims; I Love You So
(The Merry Widow Waltz); In Marsovia; Love in My Heart; Maxim's;
Silly, Silly Cavalier; Vilia
cast: Ethel Jackson, Donald Brian, Lois Ewell, R. E. Graham, William
Weedon, Fred Frear

1908   *Notable Musical Openings of the Year:*

THE THREE TWINS
music by Karl Hoschna, lyrics by Otto Harbach, book by Charles Dickson,
adapted from a farce by R. Pancheco
opened on Broadway 6/15/08 for a run of 288 performances
selected songs: Cuddle Up a Little Closer; Goodnight Sweetheart;
Over There; Yama-Yama Man
cast: Fred Allen, Libby Holman, Clifton Webb, Tamara Geva,
Fred MacMurray

THE ZIEGFELD FOLLIES OF 1908
music by Maurice Levi and various composers, lyrics & book mainly
by Harry B. Smith
opened on Broadway 6/15/08 for a run of 120 performances
cast: Nora Bayes, Grace La Rue, Harry Watson, Mlle. Dazie

SPORTING DAYS (A Hippodrome Extravaganza)
music by Manuel Klein, lyrics & book by Manuel Klein &
Edward P. Temple
opened on Broadway 9/4/08 for a run of 477 performances

1909   *Notable Musical Openings of the Year:*

THE FAIR CO-ED
music by Gustav Luders, lyrics & book by George Ade
opened on Broadway 2/1/09 for a run of 136 performances
selected songs: Here in the Starlight; I'll Dream of the Sweet Co-ed;
A Little Girl That's Wise
cast: Elsie Janis, Arthur Stanford

THE ZIEGFELD FOLLIES OF 1909
music by Maurice Levi and various composers, lyrics & book mainly by
Harry B. Smith
opened on Broadway 6/14/09 for a run of 64 performances
cast: Lilliam Lorraine, Nora Bayes, Bessie Clayton, Jack Norworth,
Mae Murray, Eve Tanguay

A TRIP TO JAPAN (A Hippodrome Extravaganza)
music & lyrics by Manuel Klein, book by R. H. Burnside
opened on Broadway 9/4/09 fir a run of 447 performances

THE CHOCOLATE SOLDIER
music by Oscar Straus, lyrics & book by Stanislaus Stange
opened on Broadway 9/13/09 for a run of 296 performances
selected songs: Falling In Love; The Letter Song; My Hero; Seek the Spy;
Sympathy; Thank the Lord the War Is Over; That Would Be Lovely
cast: Ida Brooks Hunt, J. E. Gardner, Flavia Arcaro, William Pruette

1910 *Featured Song Selection:*
Italian Street Song
from *Naughty Marietta*

Notable Musical Openings of the Year:

SUMMER WIDOWERS
music by A. Baldwin Sloane, lyrics & book by Glen MacDonough
opened on Broadway 6/4/10 for a run of 140 performances
selected songs: I'd Like to Furnish a Flat for You; On the Boardwalk;
Those Were the Happy Days

THE ZIEGFELD FOLLIES OF 1910
music by gus Edwards and various composers, lyrics & book
mainly by Harry B. Smith
opened on Broadway 6/20/10 for a run of 88 performances

MADAME SHERRY
music by Karl Hoschna, lyrics & book by Otto Harbach
opened on Broadway 8/30/10 for a run of 231 performances
selected songs: The Birth of Passion; Every Little Movement; I Want to
Play House With You; Put Your Arms Around Me Honey; The Smile She
Meant for Me
cast: Lina Abarbanell, Ralph Herz, Elizabeth Murray, Jack Gardner,
Dorothy Jardon, Frances Demarest

THE INTERNATIONAL CUP AND THE BALLET OF NIAGARA
(A Hippodrome Extravaganza)
music & lyrics by Manuel Klein, book by R. H. Burnside
opened on Broadway 9/3/10 for a run of 333 performances

NAUGHTY MARIETTA
Music by Victor Herbert, book & lyrics by Rida Johnson Young
opened on Broadway 11/7/10 for a run of 136 performances
selected songs: Ah! Sweet Mystery of Life; I'm Falling in Love With
Someone; Italian Street Song; Live for Today; Naughty Marietta; 'Neath the
Southern Moon; Tramp! Tramp! Tramp!
cast: Emma Trentini, Orville Harrold, Edward Martindel, Marie Duchene,
Peggy Wood

1911 *Featured Song Selection:*
Woodman, Woodman, Spare That Tree
from *Ziegfeld Follies of 1911*

Notable Musical Openings of the Year:

THE HEN PECKS
music by A. Baldwin Sloane, lyrics by E. Ray Goetz, book by
Glen MacDonough
opened on Broadway 2/4/11 for a run of 137 performances
selected songs: It's a Skirt; June; Little Italy; White Light Alley
cast: Lew Fields, Lawrence Wheat, Vernon Castle, Gertrude Quinlan,
Blossom Seeley, Ethel Johnson

THE PINK LADY
music by Ivan Caryll, lyrics & book by C. M. S. McLellan
opened on Broadway 3/13/11 for a run of 312 performances
selected songs: Donny Did, Donny Didn't; Hide and Seek; My Beautiful
Lady; On the Saskatchewan
cast: Hazel Dawn, Alice Dovey, William Elliott, Frank Lalor, Jed Prouty

LA BELLE PAREE
music by Frank Tours & Jerome Kern, lyrics by Edward Madden, book by
Edgar Smith
opened on Broadway 3/20/11 for a run of 104 performances
cast: Harry Fisner, Stella Mayhew, Melville Ellis, George White,
Kitty Gordon, Al Jolson

THE ZIEGFELD FOLLIES OF 1911
music by Maurice Levi, Raymond Hubbell, Irving Berlin and various
composers, lyrics & book by George V. Hobart and various others
opened on Broadway 6/26/11 for a run of 80 performances
cast: Bessie McCoy, Leon Errol, The Dolly Sisters, Bert Williams,
Lillian Lorraine, Fanny Brice

AROUND THE WORLD (A Hippodrome Extravaganza)
music & lyrics by Manuel Klein, book by Carroll Fleming
opened on Broadway 9/2/11 for a run of 445 performances

THE LITTLE MILLIONAIRE
music, lyrics & book by George M. Cohan
opened on Broadway 9/25/11 for a run of 192 performances
selected songs: Barnum Had the Right Idea; Musical Moon; Oh, You
Wonderful Girl; We Do All the Dirty Work
cast: George M. Cohan, Jerry Cohan, Helen Cohan, Donald Crisp

VERA VIOLETTA
music by Louis A. Hirsch, Edmund Eysler and others (with interpolations),
book by Harold Atteridge & Leonard Liebling, adapted from a German play
by Leo Stein
opened on Broadway 12/20/11 for a run of 112 performances
selected songs: Come and Dance with Me; The Gaby Glide; Olga from the
Volga; Ta-ra-ra-bom-de-re; When You Hear Love's Hello
cast: Al Jolson, Gaby Deslys, Harry Pilcer, Jose Collins

1912 *Featured Song Selection:*
Giannina Mia
from *The Firefly*

Notable Musical Openings of the Year:

HOKEY POKEY (A Weber and Fields Extravaganza)
music by John Stromberg, lyrics & book by Edgar Smith & E. Ray Goetz
opened on Broadway 2/8/12 for a run of 108 performances
cast: Weber and Fields, William Collier, Lillian Russell, Fay Templeton,
Ada Lewis, Bessie Clayton

WALL STREET GIRL
music by Karl Hoschna, lyrics Hapgood Burt, book by Margaret Mayo &
Edgar Selwyn
opened on Broadway 4/15/12 for a run of 56 performances
selected songs: I Want a Regular Man
cast: William P. Carleton, Harry Gilfoil, Charles Winniger, Will Rogers,
Blanch Ring

OH! OH! DELPHINE
music by Ivan Caryll, lyrics & book by C. M. S. McLellan (Henry Morton),
based on a French farce
opened on 9/30/12 for a run of 248 performances
selected songs: Everything's At Home Except Your Wife; Venus Waltz;
Why Shouldn't You Tell Me That?
cast: Octavia Broske, Frank McIntyre, Frank Doane, Grace Edmond

THE ZIEGFELD FOLLIES OF 1912
music by Raymond Hubbell and others, lyrics & book mainly by
Harry B. Smith
opened on Broadway 10/21/12 for a run of 88 performances

THE FIREFLY
music by Rudolf Friml, lyrics & book by Otto Harbach
opened on Broadway 12/2/12 for a run of 120 performances
selected songs: Giannina Mia; Love Is Like a Firefly; Sympathy; When a
Maid Comes Knocking at Your Heart
cast: Emma Trentini, Craig Campbell, Roy Atwell, Sammy Lee,
Audrey Maple, Melville Stewart

1913 *Notable Musical Openings of the Year:*

THE ZIEGFELD FOLLIES OF 1913
music by Raymond Hubbell, Dave Stampler and various composers, lyrics &
book by George V. Hobart, Gene Buck and various writers
opened on Broadway 6/16/13 for a run of 96 performances
cast: Ann Pennington, Leon Errol, Frank Tinney

SWEETHEARTS
music by Victor Herbert, lyrics by Robert B. Smith, book by Harry B. Smith
& Mark Luescher
opened on Broadway 9/8/13 for a run of 136 performances
selected songs: Angelus; Every Lover Must Meet His Fate; Jeanette and Her
Little Wooden Shoes; Pretty as a Picture; Sweethearts
cast: Christie MacDonald, Thomas Conkey, Ethel Du Fre Houston,
Edwin Wilson, Tom McNaughton

HIGH JINKS
music by Rudolf Friml, book by Otto Haverbach (Harbach) &
Leo Dietrichstein
opened on 12/10/13 for a run of 213 performances
selected songs: Something Seems Tingle-Ingleing; When Sammy Sang the
Marseillaise
cast: Elizabeth Murray, Tom Lewis, Elaine Hammerstein

1914

Featured Song Selection:
They Didn't Believe Me
from *The Girl From Utah*

Notable Musical Openings of the Year:

THE GIRL FROM UTAH
music by Jerome Kern & various composers, lyrics by
Harry B. Smith & various writers, book by James T. Tanner
& Harry B. Smith
opened on Broadway 8/24/14 for a run of 120 performances
selected songs: Gilbert the Filbert; The Land of Let's
Pretend; Same Sort of Girl; They Didn't Believe Me; Why
Don't They Dance the Polka?
cast: Julia Sanderson, Donald Brian, Joseph Cawthorn,
Queenie Vassar, Venita Fitzhugh

CHIN-CHIN
music by Ivan Caryll, lyrics by Anne Caldwell &
James O'Dea, book by Anne Caldwell & R. H. Burnside
opened on Broadway 10/20/14 for a run of 295 performances
selected songs: Goodbye Girls I'm Through; It's a Long
Way to Tipperary; Love Moon; The Mulberry Tree; Violet
cast: David Montgomery, Fred Stone, Helen Falconer,
Douglas Stevenson

THE ONLY GIRL
music by Victor Herbert, lyrics by Henry Blossom, book by
Henry Blossom, adapted from Our Wives by Frank Mandel
opened on Broadway 11/2/14 for a run of 240 performances
selected songs: When You're Away; When You're Wearing
the Ball and Chain; Why Should We Stay Home and Sew?;
You're the Only Girl for Me
cast: Wilda Bennett, Thurston Hall, Adele Rowland

WATCH YOUR STEP
music & lyrics by Irving Berlin, book by Harry B. Smith
opened on Broadway 12/8/14 for a run of 175 performances
selected songs: Play a Simple Melody; Settle Down in a
One-Horse Town; The Syncopated Walk; They Always
Follow Me Around; When I Discovered You
cast: Vernon & Irene Castle, Frank Tinney, Charles King,
Elizabeth Brice, Elizabeth Murray, Harry Kelly,
Justine Johnstone

1915

Featured Song Selection:
I Love a Piano
from *Stop! Look! Listen!*

Notable Musical Openings of the Year:

ZIEGFELD FOLLIES OF 1915
music by Louis A. Hirsch, lyrics by Gene Buck, sketches by Gene Buck,
Rennold Wolf & Channing Pollock
opened on Broadway 6/21/15 for a run of 104 performances
selected songs: A Girl For Each Month of the Year; Hello, Frisco!; Hold Me
in Your Loving Arms; I Can't Do Without Girls
cast: W. C. Fields, Ann Pennington. Mae Murray, Leon Errol, Bert Williams,
George White, Ed Wynn, Ina Claire

THE BLUE PARADISE
music by Sigmund Romberg & Edmund Eysler, lyrics by Herbert Reynolds,
book by Edgar Smith
opened on Broadway 8/5/15 for a run of 356 performances
selected songs: Auf Wiedersehn; One Step Into Love; A Toast to Woman's
Eyes, Vienna, Vienna
cast: Vivienne Segal, Cecil Lean, Cleo Mayfield, Ted Lorraine, Robert Pitkin,
Frances Demarest, Teddy Webb

VERY GOOD EDDIE
music by Jerome Kern & various composers, lyrics by Schuyler Greene &
various writers, book by Philip Bartholomae & F. Ray Comstock
opened on Broadway 12/23/15 for a run of 341 performances
selected songs: Babes in the Wood; Isn't It Great to Be Married?; Nodding
Roses; Old Boy Neutral; On the Shore at Le Lei Wi; Some Sort of
Somebody; Thirteen Collar
cast: Ernest Truex, Alice Dovey, Oscar Shaw, Helen Raymond,
John E. Hazzard, John Willard, Ada Lewis

STOP! LOOK! LISTEN!
music & lyrics by Irving Berlin, book by Harry B. Smith
opened on Broadway 12/25/15 for a run of 105 performances
selected songs: Everything in America is Ragtime; I Love a Piano; When I
Get Back to the U. S. A.
cast: Gaby Deslys, Harland Dixon, Harry Fox, Harry Pilcer

1916

Notable Musical Openings of the Year:

ROBINSON CRUSOE JR.
music by Sigmond Romberg and various others, lyrics by Harold Atteridge
and various writers, book by Harold Atteridge
opened on Broadway 2/17/16 for a run of 139 performances
selected songs: My Voodoo Lady; Where Did Robinson Crusoe Go with
Friday on Saturday Night?; Where the Black-Eyed Susans Grow; Yacka
Hula Hickey Dula
cast: Al Jolson, Kitty Doner, Claude Flemming, Lawrence D'Orsay

THE ZIEGFELD FOLLIES OF 1916
music by Louis A. Hirsch, lyrics & book by George V. Hobart, Gene Buck
and various writers
opened on Broadway 6/12/16 for a run of 112 performances
cast: Ina Claire, Bert Williams, Marion Davies, Ann Pennington, Fanny Brice,
W. C. Fields

THE BIG SHOW (A Hippodrome Extravaganza)
music by Raymond Hubbell, lyrics by John L. Golden, book by R. H. Burnside
opened on Broadway 8/31/16 for a run of 425 performances

THE CENTURY GIRL
music by Victor Herbert & Irving Berlin, lyrics & book by Irving Berlin and
various unidentified authors
opened on Broadway 11/6/16 for a run of 200 performances
selected songs: Alice in Wonderland; It Takes an Irishman to Make Love;
When Uncle Sam Is the Ruler of the Sea; You Belong to Me
cast: Leon Errol, Elsie Janis, Harland Dixon, Hazel Dawn, May Leslie,
Van and Schenk, Frank Tinney

1917   *Featured Song Selection:*
Till the Clouds Roll By
from *Oh, Boy!*
Notable Musical Openings of the Year:

OH, BOY!
music by Jerome Kern, lyrics by P. G. Wodehouse, book by Guy Bolton &
P. G. Wodehouse
opened on Broadway 2/20/17 for a run of 463 performances
selected songs: The Land Where the Good Songs Go; Nesting Time in
Flatbush; An Old-Fashioned Wife; A Pal Like You; Rolled into One; 'Till
the Clouds Roll By; You Never Knew About Me

MAYTIME
music by Sigmund Romberg, lyrics & book by Rida Johnson Young &
various writers
opened on Broadway 8/16/17 for a run of 492 performances
selected songs: Dancing Will Keep You Young; Jump Jim Crow; The
Road to Paradise; Will You Remember?
cast: Peggy Wood, Charles Purcell, Ralph Herbert, William Norris,
Gertrude Vanderbilt

LEAVE IT TO JANE
music by Jerome Kern, lyrics by P. G. Wodehouse, book by Guy Bolton,
P. G. Wodehouse
opened on Broadway 8/28/17 for a run of 167 performances
selected songs: Cleopatterer; The Crickets Are Calling; Just You Watch
You Step; I'm Going to Find a Girl; Leave It to Jane; The Siren's Song;
The Sun Shines Brighter; Wait Till Tomorrow; There It Is Again
cast: Edith Hallor, Robert Pitkin, Oscar Shaw, Georgia O'Ramey

1918   *Featured Song Selection:*
Rock-a-Bye Your Baby With a Dixie Melody
from *Sinbad*

Notable Musical Openings of the Year:
OH, LADY! LADY!
music by Jerome Kern, lyrics by P. G. Wodehouse, book by Guy Bolton
& P. G. Wodehouse
opened on Broadway 2/1/18 for a run of 219 performances
selected songs: Before I Met You; Do Look at Him; Greenwich Village;
I Found You and You Found Me; Moon Song; Not Yet; When the Ships
Come Home
cast: Vivienne Segal, Carl Randall, Harry C. Browne, Carroll McComas,
Edward Abeles, Florence Shirley, Margaret Dale, Constance Binney

SINBAD
music by Sigmund Romberg & various composers, lyrics by
Harold Atteridge & various writers, book by Harold Atteridge
opened on Broadway 2/14/18 for a run of 388 performances
selected songs: Beauty and the Beast; 'N Everything; Rock-a-Bye Your
Baby With a Dixie Melody; Why Do They All Take the Night Boat to Albany?
cast: Al Jolson, Kitty Doner, Mabel Withee, Forest Huff, Grace Washburn,
Alexis Kosloff

THE ZIEGFELD FOLLIES OF 1918
music & lyrics by various writers, sketches by Gene Buck & Rennold Wolf
opened on Broadway 6/18/18 for a run of 151 performances
selected songs: Any Old Time at All; Blue Devils of France; I'm Gonna Pin
a Medal on the Girl I Left Behind; Syncopated Tune
cast: Marilyn Miller, Eddie Cantor, W. C. Fields, Will Rogers, Harry Kelly,
Ann Pennington, Lillian Lorraine, Savoy & Brennan, Fairbanks Twins

SOMETIME
music by Rudolf Friml, lyrics & book by Rida Johnson Young
opened on Broadway 10/4/18 for a run of 283 performances
selected songs: Keep on Smiling; The Tune You Can't Forget
cast: Francine Larrimore, Ed Wynn, Mae West

LISTEN LESTER
music by Harold Orlob, lyrics & book by Harry L. Cort & George E. Stoddard
opened on Broadway 12/23/18 for a run of 272 performances
selected songs: Waiting for You
cast: Johnny Dooley, Ada Lewis, Clifton Webb, Hansford Wilson,
Eddie Garvie

1919   *Featured Song Selection:*
A Pretty Girl Is Like A Melody
from *Ziegfeld Follies of 1919*

Notable Musical Openings of the Year:

ZIEGFELD FOLLIES OF 1919
music & lyrics by Irving Berlin & various composers, sketches by Gene Buck
& Rennold Wolf
opened on Broadway 6/16/19 for a run of 171 performances
selected songs: Mandy; My Baby's Arms; A Pretty Girl Is Like a Melody;
Tulip Time; You Cannot Make Your Shimmy Shake on Tea; You'd Be
Surprised
cast: Marilyn Miller, Eddie Cantor, Bert Williams, Eddie Dowling, Ray
Dooley, Johnny Dooley, Delye Alda, John Steele, Van & Schenck, Mary Hay

Ziegfeld Follies of 1919 (White)

GREENWICH VILLAGE FOLLIES
music & lyrics by various writers, sketches by John Murray Anderson &
Philip Bartholomae
opened on Broadway 7/15/19 for a run of 232 performances
selected songs: (I'll See You in) C-U-B-A; I Want a Daddy Who Will Rock
Me to Sleep; When My Baby Smiles at Me
cast: Bessie McMoy Davis, Ted Lewis Orchestra, Cecil Cunningham,
Harry K. Morton

IRENE
music by Harry Tierney, lyrics by Joseph McCarthy, book by
James Montgomery
opened on Broadway 11/18/19 for a run of 670 performances
selected songs: Alice Blue Gown; Castle of Dreams; Irene; The Last Part of
Ev'ry Party; Skyrocket
cast: Edith Day, Walter Regan, Bobbie Watson, Dorothy Walters, John Litel;
Hobart Cavanaugh, Eva Puck, Adele Rowland

1920   *Featured Song Selection:*
Look For the Silver Lining
from *Sally*

Notable Musical Openings of the Year:

TICKLE ME
music by Herbert Stothart, lyrics & book by Otto Harbach,
Oscar Hammerstein II & Frank Mandel
opened on Broadway 8/17/20 for a run of 207 performances
selected songs: If a Wish Could Make It So; Until you Say Goodbye; We've
Got Something
cast: Frank Tinney, Louise Allen, Marguerite Zander

HONEYDEW
music by Efrem Zimbalist, lyrics & book by Victor Herbert
opened on Broadway 9/6/20 for a run of 231 performances
selected songs: Believe Beloved; Drop Me a Line; The Morals of a Sailorman;
Oh How I Long for Someone
cast: Ethelind Terry, Hal Forde, Mlle. Marguerite

SALLY
music by Jerome Kern, lyrics by Clifford Grey & various writers, book by Guy Bolton
opened on Broadway 12/21/20 for a run of 570 performances
selected songs: the Church 'Round the Corner; Look for the Sliver Lining; The Lorelei; Sally; Whip-Poor-Will; Wild Rose
cast: Marilyn Miller, Leon Errol, Walter Catlett, Irving Fisher, Mary Hay, Stanley Ridges, Dolores

1921 *Featured Song Selection*
Everybody Step
from *Music Box Revue*

Notable Musical Openings of the Year:

SHUFFLE ALONG
music by Eubie Blake, lyrics by Noble Sissle, book by Flournoy Miller & Aubrey Lyles
opened on Broadway 5/23/21 for a run of 504 performances
selected songs: Bandana Days; If You've Never Been Vamped By a Brownskin; I'm Just Wild About Harry; Love Will Find a Way
cast: Flournoy Miller, Aubrey Lyles, Noble Sissle, Gertrude Saunders, Roger Matthews, Lottie Gee, Lawrence Deas, Eubie Blake

ZIEGFLED FOLLIES OF 1921
music, lyrics & sketches by various writers
opened on Broadway 6/21/21 for a run of 119 performances
selected songs: My Man; Sally, Won't You Come Back?; Second Hand Rose; Strut, Miss Lizzie
cast: Fanny Brice, W. C. Fields, Raymond Hitchcock, Ray Dooley, Mary Milburn, Van & Schenck, Florence O' Denishawn, Vera Michelena, Mary Eaton, Channing Pollack, Mary Lewis

MUSIC BOX REVUE
music & lyrics by Irving Berlin, sketches by various writers
opened on Broadway 9/22/21 for a run of 440 performances
selected songs: Everybody Step; In a Cozy Kitchenette Apartment; The Legend of Paris; My Little Book of Poetry; Say It With Music; The Schoolhouse Blues; They Call It Dancing
cast: William Collier, Wilda Bennett, Paul Frawley, Sam Bernard, Ivy Sawyer, Jospeh Stanley, Florence Moore, Brox Sisters, Chester Hale, Irving Berlin, Miriam Hodges

BLOSSOM TIME
music by Sigmund Romberg (based on Franz Schubert), lyrics & book by Dorothy Donnelly
opened on Broadway 9/29/21 for a run of 516 performances
selected songs: Serenade; Song of Love; Tell Me Daisy, Three Little Maids
cast: Bertram Peacock, Ogla Cook, Howard Marsh, Roy Cropper

1922 *Featured Song Selection:*
I'll Build a Stairway to Paradise
from *George White's Scandals*

Notable Musical Openings of the Year:

THE ZIEGFELD FOLLIES OF 1922
music by Louis A. Hirsch & David Stamper, lyrics by Gene Buck, sketches by various writers
opened on Broadway 6/5/22 for a run of 541 performances
selected songs: Mr. Gallagher and Mr. Shean; My Rambler Rose; 'Neath the South Sea Moon; Oh! Gee, Oh! Gosh, Oh! Golly, I'm, in Love
cast: Will Rogers, Gilda Gray, Gallagher and Shean, Evelyn Law, Andrew Tombes, Florence O' Denishawn, Lulu McConnell, Mary Eaton, Nervo & Knox, Mary Lewis, Alexander Gray, Jack Whiting

GEORGE WHITE'S SCANDALS OF 1922
music by George Gershwin, lyrics by B. G. De Sylva, sketches by George White & Andy Rice
opened on Broadway 8/28/22 for a run of 88 performances
selected songs: Argentina; Blue Monday Blues; Cinderelatives, I Found a Four-Leaf Clover; I'll Build a Stairway to Paradise
cast: W. C. Fields, Winnie Lightner, Paul Whiteman Orchestra, Lester Allen, George White, Jack McGowan, Pearl Regay, Dolores Costello

SALLY, IRENE AND MARY
music by J. Fred Coots, lyrics by Raymond Klages, book by Eddie Dowling & Cyrus Wood
opened on Broadway 9/4/22 for a run of 318 performances
selected songs: Do You Remember Those Days?; I Wonder Why: Time Will Tell
cast: Eddie Dowling, Jean Brown, Kitty Flynn, Edna Morn

1923 *Notable Musical Openings of the Year:*

WILDFLOWER
music by Vincent Youmans & Herbert Stothart, lyrics & book by Otto Harbach & Oscar Hammerstein II
opened on Broadway 2/7/23 for a run of 477 performances
selected songs: Bambalina; Wildflower
cast: Edith Day, Guy Robertson, Evelyn Cavanaugh

POPPY
music by Stephen Jones & Arthur Samuels, lyrics by Dorothy Donnelly & various writers, book by Dorothy Donnelly (Howard Dietz, W. C. Fleids uncredited)
opened on Broadway 9/3/23 for a run of 346 performances
selected songs: Alibi Baby; On Our Honeymoon; Two Make a Home; What Do You Do Sunday, Mary?
cast: Madge Kennedy, W. C. Fields, Robert Woolsey, Alan Edwards, Luella Gear

STEPPING STONES
music by Jerome Kern, lyrics by Anne Caldwell, book by Anne Caldwell & R.H. Burnside
opened on Broadway 11/6/23 for a run of 241 performances
selected songs: Once in a Blue Moon; Raggedy Ann
cast: Fred Stone, Allene Stone, Dorothy Stone, Jack Whiting, Oscar "Rags" Ragland, Roy Hoyer

1924   *Featured Song Selection:*
Indian Love Call
from *Rose-Marie*

Notable Musical Openings of the Year:

ANDRE CHARLOT'S REVUE OF 1924
music, lyrics & sketches by various writers
opened on Broadway 1/9/24 for a run of 298 performances
selected songs: Limehouse Blues; March With Me!; Parisian Parrot; There's Life in the Old Girl Yet; You Were Meant for Me
cast: Beatrice Lillie, Gertrude Lawrence, Jack Buchanan, Douglas Furber, Herbert Mundin, Jessie Matthews, Constance Carpenter

ROSE-MARIE
music by Rudolf Friml, Herbert Stothart, lyrics & book by Otto Harbach & Oscar Hammerstein II
opened on Broadway 9/2/24 for a run of 557 performances
selected songs: The Door of Her Dreams; Indian Love Call; The Mounties; Rose-Marie; Totem Tom-Tom; Why Shouldn't We?
cast: Mary Ellis, Dennis King, William Kent, Dorothy Makaye, Eduardo Ciannelli, Pearl Regay, Arthur Deagon

LADY, BE GOOD!
music by George Gershwin, lyrics by Ira Gershwin, book by Guy Bolton & Fred Thompson
opened on Broadway 12/1/24 for a run of 330 performances
selected songs: Fascinating Rhythm; The Half of It Dearie Blues; Hang on to Me; Little Jazz Bird; Oh, Lady Be Good; Swiss Miss
cast: Fred & Adele Astaire, Walter Catlett, Cliff Edwards, Alan Edwards, Kathleen Martyn

THE STUDENT PRINCE IN HEIDELBERG
music by Sigmund Romberg, lyrics & book by Dorothy Donnelly
opened on Broadway 12/2/24 for a run of 608 performances
selected songs: Come Boys, Let's All Be Gay, Boys (Students March Song); Deep in My Heart, Dear; Drinking Song; Golden Days; Just We Two; Serenade; To the Inn We're Marching
cast: Howard Marsh, Ilse Marvenga, Greek Evans, George Hassell, Roberta Beatty

1925   *Featured Song Selection:*
Manhattan
from *The Garrick Gaieties*

Notable Musical Openings of the Year:

THE GARRICK GAIETIES
music by Richard Rogers, lyrics by Lorenz Hart, sketches by various writers
opened on Broadway 6/8/25 for a run of 211 performances
selected songs: April Fool; Do You Love Me?; Manhattan; Old Fashioned Girl; On With the Dance; Sentimental Me
cast: Sterling Holloway, Romney Brent, Betty Starbuck, Libby Holman, June Cochrane, Edith Meiser, Philip Loeb, Sanford Meisner, Lee Strasberg

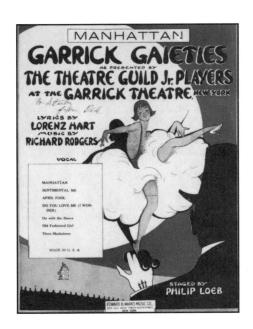

NO, NO, NANETTE
music by Vincent Youmans, lyrics by Irving Ceasar, book by Otto Harbach & Frank Mandel
opened on Broadway 9/16/25 for a run of 321 performances
selected songs: Call of the Sea; I Want to Be Happy; No, No, Nanette; Tea for Two; Too Many Rings Around Rosie; 'Where Has My Hubby Gone?' Blues; You Can Dance With Any Girl at All
cast: Louise Groody, Charles Winniger, Josephine Whittell, Wellington Cross, Eleanor Dawn, Georgia O'Ramey, Mary Lawlor, John Barker

DEAREST ENEMY
music by Richard Rodgers, lyrics by Lorenz Hart, book by Herbert Fields
opened on Broadway 9/18/25 for a run of 286 performances
selected songs: Bye and Bye; Cheerio; Here in My Arms; Here's a Kiss; I Beg Your Pardon; I'd Like To Hide It; Old Enough to Love; Sweet Peter
cast: Helen Ford, Charles Purcell, Flavia Arcaro, Harry Ford

THE VAGABOND KING
music by Rudolf Friml, lyrics by Brian Hooker, book by Brian Hooker, Russell Janney & W. H. Post
opened on Broadway 9/21/25 for a run of 511 performances
selected songs: Huguette Waltz; Love for Sale; Love Me Tonight; Nocturne; Only a Rose; Some Day; Song of the Vagabonds
cast: Dennis King, Carolyn Thomson, Max Figman, Herbert Corthell

SUNNY
music by Jerome Kern, lyrics & book by Otto Harbach & Oscar Hammerstein II
opened on Broadway 9/22/25 for a run of 517 performances
selected songs: D'Ye Love Me?; I Might Grow Fond of You; Let's Say Goodnight Till It's Morning; Sunny; Two Little Bluebirds; Who?
cast: Marilyn Miller, Jack Donahue, Clifton Webb, Mary Hay, Jospeh Cawthorn, Paul Frawley, Cliff Edwards, Pert Kelton, Moss & Fontana, Esther Howard, Dorothy Francis, George Olsen Orchestra

THE COCOANUTS
music & lyrics by Irving Berlin, book by George S. Kaufman (Morrie Ryskind uncredited)
opened on Broadway 12/8/25 for a run of 276 performances
selected songs: Florida by the Sea; A Little Bungalow; Lucky Boy; The Monkey Doodle-Doo; Why Am I a Hit With The Ladies?
cast: The Marx Brothers, Margaret Dumont, JohnBarker, Mabel Withee, Frances Williams, Brox Sisters, Basil Ruysdael, George Hale

The Cocoanuts (White)

TIP-TOES
music by George Gershwin, lyrics by Ira Gershwin, book by Guy Bolton & Fred Thompson
opened on Broadway 12/28/25 for a run of 194 performances
selected songs: Looking for a Boy; Nice Baby; Nightie Night; Sweet and Low-Down; That Certain Feeling; These Charming People; When Do We Dance?
cast: Queenie Smith, Allen Kearns, Andrew Tombes, Harry Watson Jr., Jeanette MacDonald, Robert Halliday, Gertrude McDonald

1926

Featured Song Selection:
Someone to Watch Over Me
from *Oh, Kay!*

Notable Musical Openings of the Year:

GEORGE WHITE'S SCANDALS
music by Ray Henderson, lyrics by B. G. DeSylva & Lew Brown, sketches by George White & William K. Lewis
opened on Broadway 6/14/26 for a run of 424 performances
selected songs: Birth of the Blues; Black Bottom; The Girl Is You and the Boy Is Me; Lucky Day; Rhapsody in Blue; St. Louis Blues
cast: Willie & Eugene Howard, Frances Williams, Harry Richman, Tom Patricola, Ann Pennington, McCarthy Sisters, Fairbanks Twins, Buster West, Portland Hoffa

COUNTESS MARITZA
music by Emmerich Kalman, lyrics & book by Harry B. Smith
opened on Broadway 9/18/26 for a run of 321 performances
selected songs: The Call of Love; I'll Keep on Dreaming; The One I'm Looking For; Play, Gypsies – Dance Gypsies
cast: Yvonne D'Arle, Walter Woolfe, Odette Myrtil, Carl Randall, Harry K. Morton, Vivian Hart, George Hassell

OH! KAY!
music by George Gershwin, lyrics by Ira Gershwin, book by Guy Bolton & P. G. Wodehouse
opened on Broadway 11/8/26 for a run of 256 performances
selected songs: Clap Yo' Hands; Dear Little Girl; Do Do Do; Fidgety Feet; Heaven on Earth; Maybe; Oh, Kay!; Someone to Watch Over Me
cast: Gertrude Lawrence, Oscar Shaw, Victor Moore, Harland Dixon, Fairbanks Twins, Gerald Oliver Smith, Betty Compton, Constance Carpenter

THE DESERT SONG
music by Sigmund Romberg, lyrics by Otto Harbach, & Oscar Hammerstein II, book by Otto Harbach, Oscar Hammerstein II & Frank Mandel
opened on Broadway 11/30/26 for a run of 471 performances
selected songs: The Desert Song; French Military Marching Song; I Want a Kiss; It; Let Love Go; One Alone; One Flower Grows Alone in Your Garden; The Riff Song; Romance
cast: Vivienne Segal, Robert Halliday, Eddie Buzzell, Pearl Regay, William O'Neal

1927

Featured Song Selection:
Ol' Man River
from *Show Boat*

Notable Musical Openings of the Year:

PEGGY-ANN
music by Richard Rodgers, lyrics by Lorenz Hart, book by Herbert Fields
opened on Broadway 12/27/26 for a run of 333 performances
selected songs: A Little Birdie Told Me So; Maybe It's Me; A Tree in the Park; Where's That Rainbow?
cast: Helen Ford, Lester Cole, Lulu McConnell, Betty Starbuck, Edith Meiser

RIO RITA
music by Harry Tierney, lyrics by Joseph McCarthy, book by Guy Bolton & Fred Thompson
opened on Broadway 2/2/27 for a run of 494 performances
selected songs: Following the Sun Around; If You're in Love You'll Waltz; The Kinkajou; The Ranger's Song; Rio Rita
cast: Ethelind Terry, Harold Murray, Bert Wheeler, Robert Woolsey, Ada May, Vincent Serrano

HIT THE DECK
music by Vincent Youmans, lyrics by Clifford Grey & Leo Robin, book by Herbert Fields
opened on Broadway 4/25/27 for a run of 352 performances
selected songs: Hallelujah; Harbor of My Heart; Join the Navy; Looloo; Lucky Bird; Sometimes I'm Happy; Why, Oh Why?
cast: Louise Groody, Charles King, Stella Mayhew, Madeline Cameron, Brian Donlevy, Jack McCauley

GOOD NEWS!
music by Ray Henderson, lyrics by B. G. DeSylva & Lew Brown, book by Lawrence Schwab & B. G. DeSylva
opened on Broadway 9/6/27 for a run of 551 performances
selected songs: The Best Things in Life Are Free; Good News; He's a Ladies Man; Just Imagine; Lucky in Love; The Varsity Drag
cast: Mary Lawlor, John Price Jones, Gus Shy, Inez Courtney, Zelma O'Neal, George Olsen Orchestra

A CONNECTICUT YANKEE
music by Richard Rodgers, lyrics by Lorenz Hart, book by Herbert Fields
opened on Broadway 11/3/27 for a run of 418 performances
selected songs: I Feel at Home With You; My Heart Stood Still; On a Desert Island With Thee; Thou Swell
cast: William Gaxton, Constance Carpenter, Nana Bryant, June Cochrane, William Norris, Jack Thompson

FUNNY FACE
music by George Gershwin, lyrics by Ira Gershwin, book by Paul Gerard Smith & Fred Thompson
opened on Broadway 11/22/27 for a run of 244 performances
selected songs: The Babbitt and the Bromide; Funny Face; He Loves and She Loves; High Hat; Let's Kiss and Make Up; My One and Only; 'S Wonderful
cast: Fred & Adele Astaire, Victor Moore, William Kent, Allen Kearns, Betty Compton, Dorothy Jordan

SHOW BOAT
music by Jerome Kern, lyrics & book by Oscar Hammerstein II
opened on Broadway 12/27/27 for a run of 572 performances
selected songs: After The Ball (interpolated); Can't Help Lovin' Dat Man; Life Upon the Wicked Stage; Make Believe; Ol' Man River; Why Do I Love You; You Are Love; Bill
cast: Charles Winninger, Norma Terris, Howard Marsh, Helen Morgan, Jules Bledsoe, Edna May Oliver, Eva Puck, Sammy White, Tess Gardella, Charles Ellis, Francis X. Mahoney

1928

Featured Song Selection:
I Can't Give You Anything But Love
from *Blackbirds of 1928*

Notable Musical Openings of the Year:

ROSALIE
music by George Gershwin & Sigmund Romberg, lyrics by Ira Gershwin & P. G. Wodehouse, book by William Anthony McGuire & Guy Bolton
opened on Broadway 1/10/28 for a run of 335 performances
selected songs: Ev'rybody Knows I Love Somebody; How Long Has This Been Going On?; Oh Gee! Oh Joy!; Say So!; West Point Song
cast: Marilyn Miller, Jack Donohue, Frank Morgan, Margaret Dale, Bobbe Arnst, Oliver McLennan

THE THREE MUSKETEERS
music by Rudolf Friml, lyrics by Clifford Grey, book by William Anthony McGuire
opened on Broadway 3/13/28 for a run of 318 performances
selected songs: Ma Belle; March of the Musketeers; My Sword and I; One Kiss; Queen of My Heart; Your Eyes
cast: Dennis King, Vivienne Segal, Lester Allen, Vivienne Osborne, Yvonne D'Arle, Reginald Owen, Joseph McCauley, Harriet Hoctor, Douglass Dumbrille, Detmar Poppen, Clarence Derwent

BLACKBIRDS OF 1928
music by Jimmy McHigh, lyrics by Dorothy Fields, sketches (uncredited)
opened on Broadway 5/9/28 for a run of 518 performances
selected songs: Diga Diga Doo; Doin' the New Low-Down; I Can't Give You Anything But Love; I Must Have That Man; Porgy
cast: Adelaide Hall, Bill Robinson, Aida Ward, Tim Moore, Elizabeth Welch, Mantan Moreland, Cecil Mack, Hall Johnson Choir

THE NEW MOON
music by Sigmund Romberg, lyrics by Oscar Hammerstein II, book by Oscar Hammerstein II, Frank Mandel & Laurence Schwab
opened on Broadway 9/19/28 for a run of 509 performances
selected songs: Lover, Come Back To Me; Marianne; One Kiss; Softly, as in a Morning Sunrise; Stouthearted Men; Wanting You
cast: Evelyn Herbert, Robert Halliday, Gus Shy, Max Figman, William O'Neal

HOLD EVERYTHING!
music by Ray Henderson, lyrics by B. G. DeSylva & John McGowan
opened on Broadway 10/10/28 for a run of 413 performances
selected songs: Don't Hold Everything; To Know You Is to Love You; Too Good to Be True; You're the Cream in My Coffee
cast: Jack Whiting, Ona Munson, Bert Lahr, Betty Compton, Victor Moore, Nina Olivette, Frank Allworth, Gus Schilling

WHOOPEE
music by Walter Donaldson, lyrics by Gus Kahn, book by William Anthony McGuire
opened on Broadway 12/4/28 for a run of 379 performances
selected songs: I'm Bringing a Red Red Rose; Love Me or Leave Me; Makin' Whoopee; Until You Get Somebody Else
cast: Eddie Cantor, Ruth Etting, Ethel Shutta, Paul Gregory, Frances Upton, Tamara Geva, Albert Hackett, George Olsen Orchestra, Buddy Ebsen

1929

Featured Song Selection:
Why Was I Born?
from *Sweet Adeline*

Notable Musical Openings of the Year:

FOLLOW THRU
music by Ray Henderson, lyrics by B. G. DeSylva & Lew Brown, book by Laurence Schwab & Frank Mandel
opened on Broadway 1/9/29 for a run of 403 performances
selected songs: Button Up Your Overcoat; I Want To Be Bad; My Lucky Star; You wouldn't Fool Me Would You?
cast: Jack Haley, Zelma O'Neal, Irene Delroy, Eleanor Powell, Madeline Cameron, John Barker

THE LITTLE SHOW
music by Arthur Schwartz & various composers, lyrics by
Howard Dietz & various writers, book by Howard Dietz,
George S. Kaufman & various writers
opened on Broadway 4/30/29 for a run of 321 performances
selected songs: Can't We Be Friends?; Hammacher-
Schlemmer, I Love You; I Guess I'll Have to Change My
Plan; I've Made a Habit of You; A Little Hut in Hoboken;
Moanin' Low
cast: Clifton Webb, Fred Allen, Libby Holman, Romney
Brent, Portland Hoffa, Bettina Hall, Jack McCauley,
Peggy Conklin, Constance Cummings

SWEET ADELINE
music by Jerome Kern, lyrics by Oscar Hammerstein II,
book by Arthur Hammerstein
opened on Broadway 9/3/29 for a run of 234 performances
selected songs: Don't Ever Leave Me; Here Am I; Some
Girls on Your Mind; The Sun About to Rise; 'Twas Not So
Long Ago; Why Was I Born?
cast: Helen Morgan, Charles Butterworth, Irene Franklin,
Robert Chisholm, Violet Carlson, Max Hoffman Jr.

BITTER SWEET
music, lyrics & book by Noël Coward
opened on Broadway 11/5/29 for a run of 159 performances
selected songs: The Call of Life; Dear Little Café; If You
Could Come With Me; If Love Were All; I'll See You
Again; Ladies of the Town; Tokay; Ziguener
cast: Evelyn Lane, Gerald Nodin, Max Kirby, Mireille, John Evelyn

Three's a Crowd (Apeda)

FIFTY MILLION FRENCHMEN
music & lyrics by Cole Porter, book by Herbert Fields
opened on Broadway 11/27/29 for a run of 254 performances
selected songs: Find Me a Primitive Man; Paree, What Did You Do to Me?;
The Tale of an Oyster; You Do Something to Me; You Don't Know Paree;
You've Got That Thing
cast: William Gaxton, Genevieve Tobin, Helen Broderick, Betty Compton,
Evelyn Hoey, Jack Thompson, Thurston Hall

1930

Featured Song Selection:
Love for Sale
from *The New Yorkers*

Notable Musical Openings in the Year:

STRIKE UP THE BAND
music by George Gershwin, lyrics by Ira Gershwin, book by Morrie Ryskind
opened on Broadway 1/14/30 for a run of 191 performances
selected songs: I Mean to Say; I've Got a Crush on You; Mademoiselle in
New Rochelle; Soon; Strike Up the Band
cast: Bobby Clarke & Paul McCullough, Blanche Ring, Jerry Goff,
Doris Carson, Dudley Clements, Red Nichols Orchestra

FLYING HIGH
music by Ray Henderson, lyrics by B. G. DeSylva & Lew Brown, book by
John McGowan, B. G. DeSylva & Lew Brown
opened on Broadway 4/3/30 for a run of 357 performances
selected songs: Good for You – Bad for Me; I'll Know Him; Red Hot Chicago;
Thank Your Father; Without Love
cast: Bert Lahr, Oscar Shaw, Kate Smith, Grace Brinkley, Russ Brown,
Pearl Osgood

FINE AND DANDY
music by Kay Swift, lyrics by Paul James, book by Donald Ogden Stewart
(Joe Cook uncredited)
opened on Broadway 9/23/30 for a run of 255 performances
selected songs: Can This Be Love?; Fine and Dandy; The Jig Hop; Let's Go
Eat Worms in the Garden;
cast: Joe Cook, Neil O'Day, Dave Chasen, Eleanor Powell, Alice Boulden,
Joe Wagstaff

GIRL CRAZY
music by George Gershwin, lyrics by Ira Gershwin, book by Guy Bolton &
John McGowen
opened on Broadway 10/14/30 for a run of 272 performances
selected songs: Bidin' My Time; But Not for Me; Embraceable You; I Got
Rhythm; Sam and Delilah; Treat Me Rough
cast: Willie Howard, Allen Kearns, Ginger Rogers, William Kent,
Ethel Merman, Antonio & Renee DeMarco, Lew Parker, Roger Evans,
Red Nichols Orchestra

THREE'S A CROWD
music by Arthur Schwartz & various composers, lyrics by Howard Dietz &
various writers, sketches by various writers
opened on Broadway 10/15/30 for a run of 272 performances
selected songs: Body and Soul; Forget All Your Books; The Moment I Saw
You; Right at the Start of It; Something to Remember You By
cast: Clifton Webb, Fred Allen, Libby Holman, Tamara Geva,
Portland Hoffa, Earl Oxford, Fred MacMurray

THE NEW YORKERS
music & lyrics by Cole Porter, book by Herbert Fields
opened on Broadway 12/8/30 for a run of 168 performances
selected songs: I Happen to Like New York; Let's Fly Away; Love for Sale;
Take Me Back to Manhattan; Where Have You Been?
cast: Frances Williams, Charles King, Hope Williams, Ann Pennington,
Richard Carle, Marie Cahill, Fred Waring Orchestra, Clayton, Jackson and
Durante, Kathryn Crawford, Oscar Ragland

1931

Featured Song Selection:
Who Cares?
from *Of Thee I Sing*

Notable Musical Openings of the Year:

THE BAND WAGON
music by Arthur Schwartz, lyrics by Howard Dietz, sketches by
George S. Kaufman & Howard Dietz
opened on Broadway 6/3/31 for a run of 260 performances
selected songs: Confession; Dancing in the Dark; High and Low; Hoops; I
Love Louisa; New Sun in the Sky; Sweet Music
cast: Fred & Adele Astaire, Frank Morgan, Helen Broderick, Tilly Losch,
Philip Loeb, John Barker

EARL CARROLL VANITIES of 1931
music by Burton Lane & various composers, lyrics by Harold Anderson &
various composers, sketches by Ralph Spence & Eddie Welch
opened on Broadway 8/27/31 for a run of 278 performances
selected songs: Good Night, Sweetheart; Have a Heart; Heigh Ho, the
Gang's All Here; Tonight or Never
cast: Will Mahoney, Lillian Roth, William Demerest, Mitchell & Durant,
Milton Watson

GEORGE WHITE'S SCANDALS of 1931
music by Ray Henderson, lyrics by Lew Brown, sketches by Lew Brown,
George White & Irving Caesar
opened on Broadway 9/14/31 for a run of 202 performances
selected songs: Ladies and Gentlemen, That's Love: Life Is Just a Bowl of
Cherries; My Song; That's Why the Darkies Were Born; This Is the Missus;
The Thrill Is Gone
cast: Rudy Vallee, Ethel Merman, Willie & Eugene Howard, Everett Marshall,
Ray Bolger, Ethel Barrymore Colt, Alice Faye

THE CAT AND THE FIDDLE
music by Jerome Kern, lyrics & book by Otto Harbach
opened on Broadway 10/15/31 for a run of 395 performances
selected songs: I Watch the Love Parade; A New Love Is Old; The Night
Was Made for Love; One Moment Alone; Poor Pierrot; She Didn't Say 'Yes;
Try to Forget
cast: Georges Metaxa, Bettina Hall, Odette Myrtil, Eddie Foy Jr., José Ruben,
Lawrence Grossmith, Doris Carson, George Meader

OF THEE I SING
music by George Gershwin, lyrics by Ira Gershwin, book by George S. Kaufman
& Morrie Ryskind
opened on Broadway 12/26/31 for a run of 441 performances
selected songs: Because, Because; Hello, Good Morning; Here's a Kiss for
Cinderella; The Illegitimate Daughter; Love is Sweeping the Country; Of
thee I Sing, Baby; Who Cares?; Wintergreen for President
cast: William Gaxton, Victor Moore, Lois Moran, Grace Brinkley, June O'Dea,
George Murphy, Dudley Clements, Edward H. Robbins, Florenz Ames,
Ralph Riggs, George E. Mack

1932

Featured Song Selection:
The Song Is You
from *Music in the Air*

Notable Musical Openings of the Year:

FACE THE MUSIC
music & lyrics by Irving Berlin, book by Moss Hart
opened on Broadway 2/17/32 for a run of 165 performances
selected songs: I Say It's Spinach; Let's Have Another Cup o' Coffee; On a
Roof in Manhattan; Soft Lights and Sweet Music
cast: Mary Boland, J. Harrold Murray, Andrew Tombes, Hugh O' Connell,
Katherine Carrington, David Burns

FLYING COLORS
music by Arthur Schwartz, lyrics & sketches by Howard Dietz
opened on Broadway 9/15/32 for a run of 188 performances
selected songs: Alone Together; Louisiana Hayride; A Rainy Day; A Shine
on Your Shoes; Smokin' Reefers; Two-Faced Woman
cast: Clifton Webb, Charles Butterworth, Tamara Geva, Patsy Kelly,
Philip Loeb, Vilma & Buddy Ebsen, Larry Adler, Imogene Coca,
Monette Moore

MUSIC IN THE AIR
music by Jerome Kern, lyrics & book by Oscar Hammerstein II
opened on Broadway 11/8/32 for a run of 342 performances
selected songs: And Love Was Born; I Am So Eager; I'm, Alone; In Egern
on the Tegern Sea; I've Told Ev'ry Little Star; One More Dance; The Song
Is You; There's a Hill Beyond a Hill; We Belong Together; When the Spring
Is in the Air
cast: Reinald Werrenrath, Natalie Hall, Tullio Carminati, Katherine Carrington,
Al Shean, Walter Slezak, Nicholas Joy, Marjorie Main

TAKE A CHANCE
music by Richard A. Whiting, Nacio Herb Brown & Vincent Youmans,
lyrics by B. G. DeSylva, book by B. G. DeSylva, Lawrence Schwab &
B. G. Desylva
opened on Broadway 11/26/32 for a run of 243 performances
selected songs: Eadie Was a Lady; Rise n' Shine; Should I Be Sweet; Turn
Out the Lights; You're an Old Smoothie
cast: Jack Haley, Ethel Merman, Jack Whiting, Sid Silvers, June Knight,
Mitzie Mayfair, Oscar Ragland, Robert Gleckler

GAY DIVORCE
music & lyrics by Cole Porter, book by Dwight Taylor
opened on Broadway 11/29/32 for a run of 248 performances
selected songs: After You, Who?; How's Your Romance?; I've Got You on
My Mind; Mister and Missus Fitch; Night and Day
cast: Fred Astaire, Claire Luce, Luella Gear, Betty Starbuck, Erik Rhodes,
Eric Blore, G. P. Huntley Jr.

1933

Featured Song Selection:
Supper Time
from *As Thousands Cheer*

Notable Musical openings of the Year:

AS THOUSANDS CHEER
music & lyrics by Irving Berlin, sketches by Moss Hart
opened on Broadway 9/30/33 for a run of 400 performances
selected songs: Easter Parade; Harlem on My Mind; Heat Wave; How's
Chances?; Lonely Heart; Not for All the Rice in China; Supper Time
cast: Marilyn Miller, Clifton Webb, Helen Broderick, Ethel Waters, Hal Forde,
Jerome Cowan, Harry Stockwell, José Limon, Letitia Ide, Thomas Hamilton,
Leslie Adams

LET 'EM EAT CAKE
music by George Gershwin, lyrics by Ira Gershwin, book by Morrie Ryskind
& George S. Kaufman
opened on Broadway 10/21/33 for a run of 90 performances
selected songs: Beautifying the City; Fun to Be Fooled; Let's Take a Walk
Around the Block; The Love Song; What Can You Say in a Love Song?;
You're a Builder Upper
cast: William Gaxton, Victor Moore, Philip Loeb, Lois Moran

ROBERTA
music by Jerome Kern, lyrics & book by Otto Harbach
opened on Broadway 11/18/33 for a run of 295 performances
selected songs: I'll Be Hard to Handle; Let's Begin; Smoke Gets in Your
Eyes; Something Had to Happen; The Touch of Your Hand; Yesterdays;
You're Devastating
cast: Lyda Roberti, Bob Hope, Fay Templeton, Tamara, George Murphy,
Sydney Greenstreet, Ray Middleton, Fred MacMurray

Roberta (Vandamm)

1934

Featured Song Selection:
You're the Top
from *Anything Goes*

Notable Musical Openings of the Year:

ZIEGFELD FOLLIES of 1934
music by Vernon Duke & various composers, lyrics by E. Y. Harburg &
various writers, sketches by various writers
opened on Broadway 1/4/34 for a run of 182 performances
selected songs: I Like the Likes of You; The Last Round-Up; Suddenly;
Wagon Wheels; What Is There to Say?
cast: Fanny Brice, Willie & Eugene Howard, Everett Marshall, Jane Froman,
Vilma & Buddy Ebsen, Patricia Bowman, Cherry & June Preisser, Eve Arden,
Robert Cummings, Ina Ray Hutton

NEW FACES
music, lyrics & sketches by various writers
opened on Broadway 3/15/34 for a run of 149 performances
selected songs: The Gutter Song; Lamplight; My Last Affair; You're My
Relaxation
cast: Leonard Sillman, Imogene Coca, Nancy Hamilton, Charles Walters,
Henry Fonda, Teddy Lynch, James Shelton, Billie Heywood

LIFE BEGINS AT 8:40
music by Harold Arlen, lyrics by Ira Gershwin & E. Y. Harburg, sketches by
various writers
opened on Broadway 8/27/34 for a run of 237 performances
selected songs: Fun to Be Fooled; Let's Take a Walk Around the Block;
Things; What Can You Say in a Love Song?; You're a Builder-Upper
cast: Bert Lahr, Ray Bolger, Luella Gear, Frances Williams, Brian Donlevy,
Dixie Dunbar, Earl Oxford

THE GREAT WALTZ
music by Johann Strauss Jr., lyrics by Desmond Carter, book by Moss Hart
opened on Broadway 9/22/34 for a run of 298 performances
selected songs: Danube So Blue; Like a Star in the Sky; Love Will Find You;
While You Love Me; With All My Heart; You Are My Song
cast: Marion Claire, Marie Burke, Guy Robertson, H. Reeves-Smith,
Ernest Cossart, Alexandra Danilova

ANYTHING GOES
music & lyrics by Cole Porter, book by Guy Bolton, P. G. Wodehouse,
Howard Lindsay & Russell Crouse
opened on Broadway 11/21/34 for a run of 420 performances
selected songs: All Through the Night; Anything Goes; Be Like the Bluebeard;
Blow, Gabriel, Blow; The Gypsy in Me; I Get a Kick Out of You; There'll
Always Be a Lady Fair; You're the Top
cast: William Gaxton, Ethel Merman, Victor Moore, Bettina Hall, Vera Dunn,
Leslie Barrie, Vivian Vance, Helen Raymond, George E. Mack,
Houston Richards

1935   *Featured Song Selection:*
My Romance
from *Jumbo*

Notable Musical Openings of the Year:

AT HOME ABROAD
music by Arthur Schwartz, lyrics by Howard Dietz, sketches by
various writers
opened on Broadway 9/19/35 for a run of 198 performances
selected songs: Get Yourself a Geisha; Got a Bran' New Suit;
Hottentot Potentate; New Suit; Loadin' Time; Love Is a Dancing
Thing; Paree; Thief in the Night; What a Wonderful World
cast: Beatrice Lillie, Ethel Waters, Herb Williams, Eleanor Powell,
Paul Haakon, Reginald Gardiner, Eddie Foy Jr., Vera Allen,
John Payne

PORGY AND BESS
music by George Gershwin, lyrics by DuBose Heyward &
Ira Gershwin, book by DuBose Heyward
opened on Broadway 10/10/35 for a run of 124 performances
selected songs: Bess, You Is My Woman Now; I Got Plenty o'
Nuttin'; I Loves You, Porgy; I'm on My Way; It Ain't Necessarily
So; My Man's Gone Now; Summertime; There's a Boat Dat's
Leavin' Soon for New York; A Woman Is a Sometime Thing
cast: Todd Duncan, Anne Brown, Warren Coleman, John W.
Bubbles, Abbie Mitchell, Ruby Elzy, Georgette Harvey,
Edward Matthews, Helen Dowdy, J. Rosamond Johnson

JUBILEE
music & lyrics by Cole Porter, book by Moss Hart
opened on Broadway 10/12/35 for a run of 169 performances
selected songs: Begin the Beguine; Just One of Those Things; Me and Marie;
A Picture of Me Without You; Why Shouldn't I?
cast: Mary Boland, June Knight, Melville Cooper, Charles Walters,
Derek Williams, Mark Plant, Montgomery Clift, May Boley, Margaret Adams

JUMBO
music by Richard Rodgers, lyrics by Lorenz Hart, book by Ben Hecht &
Charles MacArthur
opened on Broadway 11/16/35 for a run of 233 performances
selected songs: The Circus Is on Parade; Little Girl Blue; The Most Beautiful
Girl in the World; My Romance; Over and Over Again
cast: Jimmy Durante, Paul Whiteman Orchestra, Donald Novis, Gloria Grafton,
A. P. Kaye, A. Robbins, Poodles Hanneford, Big Rosie, Tilda Getze

1936   *Featured Song Selection:*
There's a Small Hotel
from *On Your Toes*

Notable Musical Openings of the Year:

ZIEGFELD FOLLIES of 1936
music by Vernon Duke, lyrics by Ira Gershwin, sketches by David Freedman
opened on Broadway 1/30/36 for a run of 115 performances
selected songs: I Can't Get Started; Island in the West Indies; That Moment
of Moments; Words Without Music
cast: Fanny Brice, Bob Hope, Gertrude Niesen, Josephine Baker, Hugh
O'Connell, Harriet Hochter, Eve Arden, Judy Canova, Cherry & June Preisser,
Nicholas Brothers, John Hoysradt, Stan Kavanaugh

ON YOUR TOES
music by Richard Rodgers, lyrics by Lorenz Hart, book by
Richard Rodgers, Lorenz Hart & George Abbott
opened on Broadway 4/11/36 for a run of 315 performances
selected songs: Glad to Be Unhappy; The Heart Is Quicker
Than the Eye; It's Got to Be Love; Quiet Night; Slaughter
on Tenth Avenue (ballet); There's a Small Hotel; The
Three B's; Too Good for the Average Man
cast: Ray Bolger, Lueella Gear, Tamara Geva, Monty
Woolley, Doris Carson, David Morris, Demetrios Vilan,
George Church

RED, HOT AND BLUE!
music & lyrics by Cole Porter, book by Howard Lindsay
& Russell Crouse
opened on Broadway 10/29/36 for a run of 183 performances
selected songs: Down in the Depths (on the Nineteenth
Floor); It's De-Lovely; Ours; Red, Hot and Blue; Ridin'
High; You've Got Something
cast: Jimmy Durante, Ethel Merman, Bob Hope,
Polly Walters, Paul & Grace Hartmen, Vivian Vance,
Lew Parker

THE SHOW IS ON
music & lyrics by various writers, sketches by
David Freedman & Moss Hart
opened on Broadway 25/25/36 for a run of 237 performances
selected songs: By Strauss; Little Old Lady; Long as You've
Got Your Health; Now; Rhythm; Song of the Woodman
cast: Beatrice Lillie, Bert Lahr, Reginald Gardner, Mitzi Mayfair,
Paul Haakon, Gracie Barrie, Charles Walters, Vera Allen, Jack McCauley

Porgy and Bess (Vandamm)

1937   *Featured Song Selection:*
Where or When
from *Babes in Arms*

Notable Musical Openings of the Year:

BABES IN ARMS
music by Richard Rodgers, lyrics by Lorenz Hart, book by Richard Rodgers
& Lorenz Hart
opened on Broadway 4/14/37 for a run of 289 performances
selected songs: All at Once; Babes in Arms; I Wish I Were in Love Again;
Imagine; Johnny One Note; The Lady Is a Tramp; My Funny Valentine;
Where or When; You Are So Fair
cast: Mitzi Green, Wynn Murray, Ray Heatherton, Duke McHale,
Alfred Drake, Ray McDonald, Grace McDonald, Nicholas Brothers,
Dan Dailey

I'D RATHER BE RIGHT
music by Richard Rodgers, lyrics by Lorenz Hart, book by George S. Kaufman
& Moss Hart
opened on Broadway 11/2/37 for a run of 290 performances
selected songs: Have You Met Miss Jones?; I'd Rather Be Right; Off the
Record; Sweet Sixty-Five; We're Going to Balance the Budget
cast: George M. Cohan, Taylor Holmes, Joy Hodges, Austin Marshall,
Marion Green, Mary Jane Welsh

On Your Toes (White)

17

PINS AND NEEDLES
music & lyrics by Harold Rome, sketches by various writers
opened on Broadway 11/27/37 for a run of 1,108 performances
selected songs: Chain Store Daisy; Doin' the Reactionary; Four Little
Angels of Peace; Nobody Makes a Pass at Me; One Big Union for Two;
Sing Me a Song With Social Significance;
cast: International Ladies Garment Workers Union members

HOORAY FOR WHAT!
music by Harold Arlen, lyrics by E. Y. Harburg, book by
Howard Lindsay & Russel Crouse
opened on Broadway 1/1/37 for a run of 200 performances
selected songs: Down With Love; God's Country; In the
Shade of the New
Apple Tree; I've Gone Romantic; Moanin' in the Mornin'
cast: Ed Wynn, Jack Whiting, Paul Haakon, June Clyde,
Vivian Vance, Ruthanna Boris, Hugh Martin,
Ralph Blane, Meg Mundy

1938   *Featured Song Selection:*
September Song
from *Knickerbocker Holiday*

Notable Musical Openings of the Year:

THE CRADLE WILL ROCK
music, lyrics & book by Marc Blitzstein
opened on Broadway 1/3/38 for a run of 108 performances
selected songs: Art for Art's Sake; The Cradle Will Rock;
The Freedom of the Press; Honolulu; Joe Worker; Nickel
Under the Foot
cast: Howard DaSilva, Will Geer, Hiram Sherman,
Olive Stanton, John Hoysradt, Marc Blitzstein

I MARRIED AN ANGEL
music by Richard Rodgers, lyrics by Lorenz Hart, book by
Richard Rodgers & Lorenz Hart
opened on Broadway 5/11/38 for a run of 338 performances
cast: Dennis King, Vera Zorina, Vivienne Segal,
Walter Slezak, Audrey Christie, Charles Walters

HELLZAPOPPIN
music by Sammy Fain & various composers, lyrics by Charles Tobias and
various writers, sketches by Ole Olsen & Chic Johnson
opened on Broadway 9/22/38 for a run of 1,404 performances
selected songs: Abe Lincoln; Boomps-a-Daisy; Fuddle Dee Duddle; It's Time
to Say Aloha
cast: Ole Olsen & Chic Johnson, Barto & Mann, Radio Rogues, Hal Sherman,
Ray Kinney

KNICKERBOCKER HOLIDAY
music by Kurt Weill, lyrics & book by Maxwell Anderson
opened on Broadway 10/19/38 for a run of 168 performances
selected songs: How Can You Tell an American?; It Never Was You; The
Scars; September Song; There's Nowhere to Go But Up
cast: Walter Huston, Ray Middleton, Jeanne Maddem, Richard Kollmar,
Robert Rounsville, Howard Freeman, Clarence Nordstrom

LEAVE IT TO ME!
music & lyrics by Cole Porter, book by Bella & Samuel Spewack
opened on Broadway 11/9/38 for a run of 291 performances
selected songs: From Now On; Get Out of Town; I Want to Go Home; Most
Gentlemen Don't Like Love; My Heart Belongs to Daddy
cast: William Gaxton, Victor Moore, Sophie Tucker, Tamara, Mary Martin,
Edward H. Robins, Alexander Arso, George Tobias, Gene Kelly

THE BOYS FROM SYRACUSE
music by Richard Rodgers, lyrics by Lorenz Hart, book by George Abbott
opened on Broadway 11/23/38 for a run of 235 performances
selected songs: Falling in Love With Love; He and She; The Shortest Day of
the Year; Sing for Your Supper; This Can't Be Love; What Can You Do With
a Man?; You Have Cast Your Shadow on the Sea
cast: Jimmy Savo, Teddy Hart, Eddie Albert, Wynn Murray, Ronald Graham,
Muriel Angelus, Marcy Wescott, Betty Bruce, Burl Ives

1939   *Featured Song Selection:*
Well, Did You Evah?
from *Dubarry Was a Lady*

Notable Musical Openings of the Year:

TOO MANY GIRLS
music by Richard Rodgers, lyrics by Lorenz Hart, book by George Marion Jr.
opened on Broadway 10/18/39 for a run of 249 performances
selected songs: Give It Back to the Indians; I Didn't Know What Time It Was;
I Like to Recognize the Tune; Love Never Went to College; She Could Shake
the Maracas; Spic and Spanish
cast: Marcy Wescott, Desi Arnaz, Hal Leroy, Mary Jane Welsh, Diosa
Costello, Richard Kollmar, Eddie Bracken, Leila Ernst, Van Johnson

DUBARRY WAS A LADY
music & lyrics by Cole Porter, book by Herbert Fields & B. G. DeSylva
opened on Broadway 12/6/39 for a run of 408 performances
selected songs: But in the Morning, No; Do I Love You?; Friendship; Give
Him the Oo-la-la; It Was Written in the Stars; Katie Went to Haiti; Well,
Did You Evah?; When Love Beckoned (in Fifty-Second Street)
cast: Bert Lahr, Ethel Merman, Betty Grable, Benny Baker, Ronald Graham,
Charles Walters, Kay Sutton

DuBarry Was a Lady

1940   *Featured Song Selection:*
Bewitched
from *Pal Joey*

Notable Musical Openings of the Year:

LOUSIANA PURCHASE
music & lyrics by Irving Berlin, book by Morrie Ryskind & B. G. DeSylva
opened on Broadway 5/28/40 for a run of 444 performances
selected songs: Fools Fall in Love; It's a Lovely Day Tomorrow; Latins
Know How; The Lord Done Fixed Up My Soul; Lousiana Purchase; Outside
of That I Love You; What Chance Have I?; You Can't Brush Me Off;
You're Lonely and I'm Lonely
cast: William Gaxton, Vera Zorina, Victor Moore, Irene Bordoni, Carol Bruce,
Nick Long Jr., Hugh Martin, Ralph Blane, Edward H. Robins

CABIN IN THE SKY
music by Vernon Duke, lyrics by John Latouche, book by Lynn Root
opened on Broadway 10/25/40 for a run of 156 performances
selected songs: Cabin in the Sky; Do What You Wanna Do; Honey in the
Honeycomb; Love Turned the Light Out; My Old Virginia Home (on the
River Nile);Taking a Chance on Love
cast: Ethel Waters, Todd Duncan, Dooley Wilson, Katherine Dunham,
Rex Ingram, J. Rosamond Johnson

PANAMA HATTIE
music & lyrics by Cole Porter, book by Herbert Fields & B. G. DeSylva
opened on Broadway 10/30/40 for a run of 501 performances
selected songs: Fresh as a Daisy; I'm Throwing a Ball Tonight; I've Still
Got My Health; Let's Be Buddies; Make It Another Old-Fashioned, Please;
My Mother Would Love You
cast: Ethel Merman, Arthur Treacher, Kames Dunn, Rags Ragland,
Pat Harrington, Frank Hyers, Phyllis Brooks, Betty Hutton, Joan Carroll,
June Allyson, Lucille Bremer, Vera Ellen, Betsy Blair

PAL JOEY
music by Richard Rodgers, lyrics by Lorenz Hart, book by John O'Hara
(George Abbott uncredited)
opened on Broadway 25/25/40 for a run of 374 performances
selected songs: Bewitched; Den of Iniquity; The Flower Garden of My Heart;
Happy Hunting Horn; I Could Write a Book; Take Him; That Terrific Rainbow;
You Mustn't Kick It Around; Zip
cast: Vivienne Segal, Gene Kelly, June Havoc, Jack Durant, Leila Ernst,
Jean Casto, Van Johnson, Stanley Donen, Tilda Getze

1941

Featured Song Selection:
The Saga of Jenny
from *Lady in the Dark*

Notable Musical Openings of the Year:

LADY IN THE DARK
music by Kurt Weill, lyrics by Ira Gershwin, book by Moss Hart
opened on Broadway 1/23/41 for a run of 46 performances
selected songs: Girl of the Moment; Jenny; My Ship; One Life to Live; The
Princess of Pure Delight; This Is New; Tschaikowsky
cast: Gertrude Lawrence, Victure Mature, Danny Kaye, Macdonald Carey,
Bert Lyrtell, Evelyn Wycoff, Margaret Dale, Ron Field

BEST FOOT FORWARD
music & lyrics by Hugh Martin & Ralph Blane, book by John Cecil Holm
opened on Broadway 10/1/41 for a run of 326 performances
selected songs: Buckle Down, Winsocki; Ev'ry Time; Just a Little Joint With
a Jukebox; Shady Lady Bird; The Three B's; What Do You Think I Am?
cast: Rosemary Lane, Marty May Gil Stratton Jr., Maureen Cannon,
Nancy Walker, June Allyson, Kenny Bowers, Victoria Schools, Tommy Dix,
Danny Daniels

LET'S FACE IT
music & lyrics by Cole Porter, book by Herbert & Dorothy Fields
opened on Broadway 10/29/41 for a run of 547 performances
selected songs: A Little Rumba Numba; Ace in the Hole; Ev'rything I Love;
Farming; I Hate You, Darling; Let's Not Talk About Love; Melody in 4-F
cast: Danny Kaye, Eve Arden, Benny Baker, Mary Jane Walsh, Edith Meiser,
Vivian Vance, Nanette Fabray, Mary Parker & Billy Daniel, Jack Williams,
Houston Richards

1942

Featured Song Selection:
Nobody's Heart
from *Jupiter*

Notable Musical Openings of the Year:

BY JUPITER
music by Richard Rodgers, lyrics by Lorenz Hart, book by Richard Rodgers
& Lorenz Hart
opened on Broadway 6/3/42 for a run of 427 performances
selected songs: Careless Rhapsody; Ev'rything I've Got; Jupiter Forbid;
Life With Father; Nobody's Heart; Wait Till You See Her
cast: Ray Bolger, Constance Moore, Benay Venuta, Ronald Graham,
Bertha Belmore, Ralph Dumke, Vera Ellen, Margaret Bannerman

STAR AND GARTER (A Revue)
music, lyrics & book by various composers nd writers
opened on Broadway 6/24/42 for a run of 609 performances
selected songs: Blues in the Night; The Girl on the Police Gazette; That
Merry Wife of Windsor;
cast: Bobby Clark, Gypsy Rose Lee, Georgia Sothern, Professor Lamberti

THIS IS THE ARMY
music & lyrics by Irving Berlin, sketches (uncredited)
opened on Broadway 7/4/42 for a run of 113 performances
selected songs: American Eagles; The Army's Made a Man Out of Me; I
Left My Heart at the Stage Door Canteen; I'm Getting Tired So I Can Sleep;
Mandy; Oh, How I Hate to Get Up in the Morning; This Is the Army, Mr.
Jones; This Time
cast: Ezra Stone, Burl Ives, Gary Merrill, Julie Oshins, Robert Sidney,
Alan Manson, Earl Oxford, Nelson Barclift, Stuart Churchill, Philip Truex,
Irving Berlin

1943

Featured Song Selection:
Oh, What a Beautiful Mornin'
from *Oklahoma!*

Notable Musical Openings of the Year:

OKLAHOMA!
music by Richard Rodgers, lyrics & book by Oscar Hammerstein II
opened on Broadway 3/31/43 for a run of 2,212 performances
selected songs: All er Nothin'; The Farmer and the Cowman; I Cain't Say
No; Kansas City; Many a New Day; Oh, What a Beautiful
Mornin'; Oklahoma; Out of My Dreams; People Will Say We're in Love;
Pore Jud; The Surrey With the Fringe on Top
cast: Betty Garde, Alfred Drake, Joan Roberts, Joseph Buloff, Celeste Holm,
Howard Da Silva, Lee Dixon, Joan McCracken, Bambi Linn, George S. Irving,
George Church, Ralph Riggs, Marc Platt, Katherine Sergava

Oklahoma! (Vandamm)

THE MERRY WIDOW (Revival)
music by Franz Lehar, lyrics by Adrian Ross & Robert Gilbert, book by
Sidney Sheldon & Ben Roberts
opened on Broadway 8/4/43 for a run of 322 performances
songs: same as original production of 1907
cast: Jan Kiepura, Martha Eggerth, Melville Cooper, Ruth Matteson,
Robert Rounseville, David Wayne, Ralph Dumke, Gene Barry,
Lubov Roudenko, Milada Mladova

ONE TOUCH OF VENUS
music by Kurt Weill, lyrics by Ogden Nash, book by S. J. Perelman &
Ogden Nash
opened on Broadway 10/7/43 for a run of 567 performances
selected songs: Foolish Heart; How Much I Love You; I'm a Stranger Here
Myself; One Touch of Venus; Speak Low; That's Him; The Trouble With
Women; West Wind; Wooden Wedding
cast: Mary Martin, Kenny Baker, John Boles, Paula Laurence, Teddy Hart,
Ruth Bond, Sono Osato, Harry Clark, Allyn Ann McLerie, Helen Raymond,
Lou Wills Jr., Pearl Lang

CARMEN JONES
music by Georges Bizet, lyrics & book by Oscar Hammerstein II
opened on Broadway 12/2/43 for a run of 502 performances
selected songs: Beat Out dat Rhythm on a Drum; Dat's Love; Dere's a Café
on de Corner; Dis Flower; My Joe; Stan' Up and Fight; Whizzin' Away
Along de Track; You Talk Just Like My Maw
cast: Muriel Smith (or Inez Matthews), Luther Saxon, Carlotta Franzell,
Glenn Bryant, June Hawkins, Cosy Cole

1944

Featured Song Selection:
Lonely Town
from *On the Town*

Notable Musical Openings of the Year:

MEXICAN HAYRIDE
music & lyrics by Cole Porter, book by Herbert & Dorothy Fields
opened on Broadway 1/28/44 for a run of 481 performances
selected songs: Abracadabra; Carlotta; Count Your Blessings; Girls; I Love
You; Sing to Me, Guitar; There Must Be Someone for Me
cast: Bobby Clark, June Havoc, George Givot, Wilbur Evans, Luba Malina,
Corinna Mura, Paul Haakon, Edith Meiser, Bill Callagan, Candy Jones

FOLLOW THE GIRLS
music by Phil Charig, lyrics by Dan Shapiro & Milton Pascal, book by Guy
Bolton, Eddie Davis & Fred Thompson
opened on Broadway 4/8/44 for a run of 882 performances
selected songs: Follow the Girls; I Wanna Get Married; I'm Gonna Hang
My Hat; Twelve O'Clock and All Is Well; You're Perf
cast: Gertrude Niesen, Jackie Gleason, Buster West, Tim Herbert,
Irina Baronova, Frank Parker, William Tabbert

SONG OF NORWAY
music & lyrics by Robert Wright & George Forrest based on Edvard Grieg,
book by Milton Lazarus
opened on Broadway 8/21/44 for a run of 860 performances
selected songs: Freddy and His Fiddle; Hill of Dreams; I Love You; The
Legend; Midsummer's Eve; Now!; Piano Concerto in A Minor (instrumental);
Strange Music; Three Loves
cast: Irra Petrina, Lawrence Brooks, Robert Shafer, Helena Bliss, Sig Arno,
Alexandra Danilova, Maria Tallchief, Ruthanna Boris

BLOOMER GIRL
music by Harold Arlen, lyrics by E. Y. Harburg, book by
Sig Herzig & Fred
Sally opened on Broadway 10/5/44 for a run of 654 performances
selected songs: The Eagle and Me; Evalina; I Got a Song; It Was Good
Enough for Grandma; Right as the Rain; Sunday in Cicero Falls; T'morra,
T'morra; When the Boys Come Home
cast: Celeste Holm, David Brooks, Dooley Wilson, Joan McCracken,
Richard Huey, Margaret Douglass, Mabel Taliaferro; Matt Briggs; Herbert Ross

ON THE TOWN
music by Leonard Bernstein, lyrics & book by Betty Comden & Adolph Green
opened on Broadway 25/28/44 for a run of 463 performances
selected songs: Come Up to My Place; I Get Carried
Away; Lonely Town; Lucky to Be Me; New York, New
York; Some Other Time; Ya Got Me
cast: Sono Osato, Nancy Walker, Betty Comden,
Adolph Green, John Battles, Cris Alexander, Alice Pearce,
Allyn Ann McLerie

1945   *Featured Song Selection:*
If I Loved You
from *Carousel*

Notable Musical Openings of the Year:

UP IN CENTRAL PARK
music by Signund Romberg, lyrics by Dorothy Fields,
book by Herbert & Dorothy Fields
opened on Broadway 1/27/45 for a run of 504 performances
selected songs: April Snow; The Big Back Yard; Carousel
in the Park; Close as Pages in a Book; When You Walk in
the Room
cast: Wilbur Evans, Maureen Cannon, Betty Bruce,
Noah Beery, Maurice Burke, Charles Irwin,
Robert Rounsville

CAROUSEL
music by Richard Rodgers, lyrics & book by
Oscar Hammerstein II
opened on Broadway 4/19/45 for a run of 890 performances
selected songs: Blow High, Blow Low; Carousel Waltz
(instrumental); The Highest Judge of All; If I Loved You;
June is Bustin' Out All Over; Mr. Snow; Soliloquy;
What's the Use of Wond'rin'; When the Children Are
Asleep; You'll Never Walk Alone; You're a Queer One
Julie Jordan
cast: John Riatt, Jan Clayton, Murvyn Vye, Jean Darling,
Christine Johnson, Eric Mattson, Bambi Linn, Peter Birch,
Pearl Lang

THE RED MILL (Revival)
music by Victor Herbert, lyrics by Henry Blossom & Forman Brown,
book (uncredited)
opened on Broadway 10/16/45 for a run of 531 performances
songs: same as original production of 1906
cast: Eddie Foy Jr., Michael O'Shea, Odette Myrtil, Dorothy Stone,
Charles Collins, Ann Andre, Lorne Byron

1946   *Featured Song Selection:*
I Got the Sun in the Morning
from *Annie Get Your Gun*

Notable Musical Openings of the Year:

SHOW BOAT (Revival)
music by Jerome Kern, lyrics & book by Oscar Hammerstein II
songs: same as original production of 1927
opened 1/5/46 for a run of 418 performances
cast: Jan Clayton, Ralph Dumke, Carol Bruce, Charles Fredericks, Buddy Ebsen,
Colette Lyons, Kenneth Spencer, Pearl Primus, Talley Beatty

ST. LOUIS WOMAN
music by Harold Arlen, lyrics by Johnny Mercer, book by Arna Bontemps
& Countee Cullen
opened on Broadway 3/30/46 for a run of 113 performances
selected songs: A Woman's Perogative; Any Place I Hang My Hat Is Home;
Cakewalk Your Lady; Come Rain or Come Shine; I Had Myself a True Love;
Legalize My Name; Ridin' on the Moon
cast: Harold Nicholas, Fayard Nicholas, Pearl Bailey, Ruby Hill, Rex Ingram,
June Hawkins, Juanita Hall, Lorenzo Fuller

CALL ME MISTER
music & lyrics by Harold Rome, sketches by Arnold Auerbach &
Arnold B. Horwitt
opened on Broadway 4/18/46 for a run of 734 performances
selected songs: Along With Me; Call Me Mister; The Face on the Dime;
Goin' Home Train; Military Life; The Red Ball Express; South America,
Take It Away
cast: Betty Garrett, Jules Munshin, Bill Callahan, Lawrence Winters,
Paula Bane, Maria Karnilova, George S. Irving

ANNIE GET YOUR GUN
music & lyrics by Irving Berlin, book by Herbert & Dorothy Fields
opened on Broadway 5/16/46 for a run of 1,147 performances
selected songs: Anything You Can Do; Doin' What Comes Natur'lly; The Girl
That I Marry; I Got Lost in His Arms; I Got the Sun in the Morning; I'm an Indian
Too; Moonshine Lullaby; My Defenses Are Down; There's No Business Like
Show Business; They Say It's Wonderful; You Can't Get a Man With a Gun
cast: Ethel Merman, Ray Middleton, Marty May, Kenny Bowers, Lea Penamn,
Betty Anne Nyman, William O'Neal, Lubov Roudenko, Daniel Nagrin,
Harry Belaver, Ellen Hanley

Annie Get Your Gun (Vandamm)

1947   *Featured Song Selection:*
How Are Things in Glocca Mora?
from *Finian's Rainbow*

Notable Musical Openings of the Year:

STREET SCENE
music by Kurt Weill, lyrics by Langston Hughes, book by Elmer Rice
opened on Broadway 1/9/47 for a run of 148 performances
selected songs: Ice Cream; Moon-Faced, Starry-Eyed; Remember that I Care;
Somehow I Never Could Believe; We'll Go Away Together; What Good
Would the Moon Be?; Wouldn't You Like to Be on Broadway?; Wrapped in
a Ribbon and Tied in A Bow
cast: Norman Cordon, Anne Jeffreys, Polnya Stoska, Brian Sullivan,
Hope Emerson, Shelia Bond, Danny Daniels, Don Saxon, Juanita Hall

FINIAN'S RAINBOW
music by Burton Lane, lyrics by E. Y. Harburg, book by E.Y. Harburg &
Fred Saidy
opened on Broadway 1/10/47 for a run of 725 performances
selected songs: That Great Come-and-Get-It-Day; How Are Things in
Glocca Morra?; If This Isn't Love; Look to the Rainbow; Old Devil Moon;
Necessity; Something Sort of Grandish; When I'm Not Near the Girl I Love;
When the Idle Poor Become the Idle Rich
cast: Ella Hogan, Albert Sharpe, Donald Richards, David Wayne,
Anita Alvarez, Robert Pitkin

SWEETHEARTS (Revival)
music by Victor Herbert, lyrics by Robert B. Smith, book by John Cecil Holm
opened on Broadway 1/21/47 for a run of 288 performances
songs: 6 songs cut from original 1913 production, 2 songs added: I Might
Be Your Once-in-a-While & To the Land of My Own Romance
cast: Bobby Clarke, Marjorie Gateson, Gloria Story, Mark Dawson,
Robert Shackleton, June Knight, Cornell MacNeil

BRIGADOON
music by Frederick Loewe, lyrics & book by Alan Jay Lerner
opened on Broadway 3/13/47 for a run of 581 performances
selected songs: Almost Like Being in Love; Brigadoon; Come to Me, Bend to Me; Down on MacConnachy Square; From This Day On; The Heather on the Hill; I'll Go Home With Bonnie Jean; My Mother's Wedding Day; There but for You Go I; Waiting for My Dearie
cast: David Brooks, Marion Bell, Pamela Britton, Lee Sullivan, George Keane, James Mitchell, William Hansen, Elliott Sullivan, Helen Gallagher, Hayes Gordon, Lidija Franklin

THE MEDIUM and THE TELEPHONE
music and libretti by Gian Carlo Menotti
opened on Broadway 5/1/47 for a run of 211 performances
cast: Marie Powers, Evelyn Keller, Leo Coleman, Marilyn Cotlow

HIGH BUTTON SHOES
music by Jule Styne, lyrics by Sammy Cahn, book by Stephen Longstreet (George Abbott & Phil Silvers uncredited)
opened on Broadway 10/9/47 for a run of 727 performances
selected songs: Can't You Just See Yourself?; I Still Get Jealous; On a Sunday by the Sea; Papa, Won't You Dance With Me?; You're My Girl
cast: Phil Silvers, Nanette Fabray, Jack McCauley, Mark Dawson, Joey Faye, Lois Lee, Sondra Lee, Helen Gallagher, Nathaniel Frey, Johnny Stewart, Paul Godkin

ALLEGRO
music by Richard Rodgers, lyrics & book by Oscar Hammerstein II
opened on Broadway 10/10/47 for a run of 315 performances
selected songs: Allegro; A Fellow Needs a Girl; The Gentleman Is a Dope; Money Isn't Ev'rything; So Far; You Are Never Away
cast: John Battles, Annamary Dickey, William Ching, John Conte, Muriel O'Malley, Lisa Kirk, Roberta Jonay

1948 *Featured Song Selection:*
Brush Up Your Shakespeare
from *Kiss Me, Kate*

Notable Musical Openings of the Year:

MAKE MINE MANHATTAN
music by Richard Lewine, lyrics & sketches by Arnold B. Horwitt
opened on Broadway 1/15/48 for a run of 429 performances
selected songs: Gentleman Friend; I Fell in Love With You; My Brudder and Me; Phil the Fiddler; Saturday Night in Central Park
cast: Sid Caesar, David Burns, Sheila Bond, Joshua Shelley, Kyle McDonnell, Danny Daniels, Nelle Fisher, Ray Harrison, Jack Kilty, Larry Carr

INSIDE U.S.A.
music by Arthur Schwartz, lyrics by Howard Dietz, book by Arnold Auerbach, Arnold B. Horwitt & Moss Hart
opened on Broadway 4/30/48 for a run of 399 performances
selected songs: At the Mardi Gras; Blue Grass; First Prize at the Fair; Haunted Heart; Inside U.S.A.; My Gal is Mine Once More; Rhode Island is Famous for You
cast: Beatrice Lillie, Jack Haley, John Tyers, Herb Shriner, Valerie Bettis, Lewis Nye, Carl Reiner, Thelma Carpenter, Estelle Loring, Eric Victor, Talley Beatty, Jack Cassidy

LOVE LIFE
music by Kurt Weill, lyrics & book by Alan Jay Lerner
opened on Broadway 10/7/48 for a run of 252 performances
selected songs: Economics; Green-Up Time; Here I'll Stay; I Remember It Well; Mr. Right; Progress
cast: Nanette Fabray, Ray Middleton, Johnny Stewart, Cheryl Archer, Jay Marshall

WHERE'S CHARLEY?
music & lyrics by Frank Loesser, book by George Abbott
opened on Broadway 10/11/48 for a run of 792 performances
selected songs: At the Red Rose Cotillion; Lovlier Than Ever; Make a Miracle; My Darling, My Darling; The New Ashmoleon Marching Society and Student's Conservatory Band; Once in Love With Amy
cast: Ray Bolger, Allyn Ann McLerie, Byron Palmer, Doretta Morrow, Horace Cooper, Jane Lawrence, Paul England, Cornell MacNeil

AS THE GIRLS GO
music by Jimmy McHugh, lyrics by Harold Adamson, book by William Roos
opened on Broadway 11/13/48 for a run of 420 performances
selected songs: As the Girls Go; Father's Day; Lucky in the Rain; There's No Getting Away from You; You Say the Nicest Things, Baby
cast: Bobby Clark, Irene Rich, Bill Callahan, Kathryn Lee, Betty Jane Watson, Hobart Cavanaugh, Betty Lou Barto, Dick Dana, Gregg Sherwood, Jo Sullivan, Buddy Schwab

LEND AN EAR
music, lyrics & sketches by Charles Gaynor
opened on Broadway 12/16/48 for a run of 460 performances
selected songs: Doin' the Old Yahoo Step; Give Your Heart a Chance to Sing; Molly O'Reilly; Who Hit Me?
cast: William Eyhte, Carol Channing, Yvinne Adair, Gene Nelson, Jennie Lou Law, Gloria Hamilton, Bob Scheerer

KISS ME, KATE
music & lyrics by Cole Porter, book by Samuel & Bella Spewack
opened on Broadway 12/30/48 for a run of 1, 070 performances
Always True to You in My Fashion; Another Op'nin', Another Show; Bianca; Brush Up Your Shakespeare; I Am Ashamed That Women Are So Simple; I Hate Men; I've Come to Wive It Wealthily in Padua; So in Love; Tom, Dick or Harry; Too Darn Hot; We Open in Venice; Were Thine That Special Face; Why Can't You Behave?; Wunderbar; Where Is the Life That Late I Led?
cast: Alfred Drake, Patricia Morison, Harold Lang, Lisa Kirk, Harry Clark, Jack Diamond, Annabelle Hill, Lorenzo Fuller, Marc Breaux

Kiss Me, Kate (Eileen Darby)

1949 *Featured Song Selection:*
Some Enchanted Evening
from *South Pacific*

Notable Musical Openings of the Year:

SOUTH PACIFIC
music by Richard Rodgers, lyrics by Oscar Hammerstein II, book by Oscar Hammerstein II & Joshua Logan
opened on Broadway 4/7/49 for a run of 1,925 performances
selected songs: Bali Ha'i; Bloody Mary; A Cockeyed Optimist; Happy Talk: Honey Bun; I'm Gonna Wash That Man Right Outa My Hair; Some Enchanted Evening; There Is Nothin' Like a Dame; This Nearly Was Mine; A Wonderful Guy; Younger Than Springtime; You've Got to Be Carefully Taught
cast: Mary Martin, Ezio Pinza, Myron McMormick, Juanita Hall, William Tabbert, Betta St. John, Martin Wolfson, Harvey Stephens, Richard Eastham, Henry Slate, Fred Sadoff, Archie Savage

MISS LIBERTY
music & lyrics by Irving Berlin, book by Robert E. Sherwood
opened on Broadway 7/15/49 for a run of 308 performances
selected songs: Give Me Your Tired, Your Poor; Homework; Just
One Way to Say I Love You; Let's Take an Old-Fashioned Walk ;
Little Fish in a Big Pond; Only for Americans; Paris Wakes Up
and Smiles;You Can Have Him
cast: Eddie Albert, allyn Ann McLerie, Mary McCarty;
Charles Dingle, Philip Bourneuf, Ethel Griffies, Herbert Berghof,
Tommy Rall, Janice Rule, Maria Karnilova, Dody Goodman

LOST IN THE STARS
music by Kurt Weill, lyrics & book by Maxwell Anderson
opened on Broadway 10/30/49 for a run of 273 performances
selected songs: Big Mole; A Bird of Passage; Cry, the Beloved
Country; The Hills of Ixipo; The Little Grey House; Lost in the
Stars; Stay Well; Thousands of Miles; Train to Johannesburg;
Trouble Man
cast: Todd Duncan, Leslie Banks, Warren Coleman, Inez Matthews,
Julian Mayfield, Frank Roane, Sheila Guyse, Herbert Coleman

REGINA
music and words by Marc Blitzstein
opened 10/31/93 for a run of 56 performances
selected numbers: The Best Thing of All; What Will It Be for Me?:
Music, Music, Music; Gallantry; The Rain Quartet; Greedy Girl
cast: Jane Pickens, Brenda Lewis, Priscilla Gillette,
William Wilderman, and Carol Brice

GENTLEMEN PREFER BLONDES
music by Jule Styne, lyrics by Leo Robin, book by Josepf Stein & Anita Loos
opened on Broadway 12/8/49 for a run of 740 performances
selected songs: Bye Bye Baby; Diamonds Are a Girl's Best Friend; It's
Delightful Down in Chile; Just a Kiss Apart; A Little Girl from Little Rock
cast: Carol Channing, Yvonne Adair, Jack McCauley, Eric Brotherson,
Alice Pearce, Rex Evans, Anita Alvarez, George S. Irving, Mort Marshall,
Howard Morris, Charles "Honi" Coles, Cholly Atkins

1950   *Featured Song Selection:*
Luck Be a Lady
from *Guys and Dolls*

Notable Musical Openings of the Year:

THE CONSUL
music and words by Gian Carlo Menotti
opened 3/15/50 for a run of 269 performances
cast: Marie Powers, Patricia Neway, Cornell MacNeill

MICHAEL TODD'S PEEP SHOW
music and lyrics by various writers, sketches by Bobby Cark, H.I. Phillips,
William Roos, Billy Wells
opened 6/28/50 for a run of 278 performances

CALL ME MADAM
music & lyrics by Irving Berlin, book by Howard Lindsay & Russel Crouse
opened on Broadway 10/12/50 for a run of 644 performances
selected songs: The Best Thing for You; Can You Use Any Money Today?;
The Hostess With the Mostes' on the Ball; It's a Lovely Day Today;
Marrying for Love; They Like Ike; You're Just in Love
cast: Ethel Merman, Paul Lukas, Russell Nype, Galina Talva, Pat Harrington,
Alan Hewitt, Tommy Rall, Nathaniel Frey

GUYS AND DOLLS
music & lyrics by Frank Loesser, book by Abe Burrows
opened on Broadway 11/24/50 for a run of 1,200 performances
selected songs: Adelaide's Lament; A Bushel and a Peck; Follow the Fold;
Fugue for Tinhorns; Guys and Dolls; If I Were a Bell; I'll Know; I've Never
Been in Love Before; Luck Be a Lady; Marry the Man Today; More I Cannot
Wish You; My Time of Day; The Oldest Established; Sit Down, You're
Rockin' the Boat; Sue Me; Take Back Your Mink
cast: Robert Alda, Vivian Blaine, Sam Levene, Isabel Bigley, Pat Rooney Sr.,
B. S. Pully, Stubby Kaye, Tom Pedi, Johnny Silver, Peter Gennaro, Onna White,
Buddy Schwab

1951   *Featured Song Selection:*
Hello, Young Lovers
from *The King and I*

Notable Musical Openings of the Year:

THE KING AND I
music by Richard Rodgers, lyrics & book by Oscar Hammerstein II
opened on Broadway 3/29/51 for a run of 1,246 performances
selected songs: Getting to Know You; Hello, Young Lovers; I Have Dreamed;
I Whistle a Happy Tune; March of the Siamese Children (instrumental); My
Lord and Master; A Puzzlement; Shall I Tell You What I Think of You?;
Shall We Dance?; Something Wonderful; We Kiss in a Shadow
cast: Gertrude Lawrence, Yul Brenner, Dorothy Sarnoff, Doretta Morrow,
Larry Douglas, Johnny Stewart, Sandy Kennedy, Lee Becker Theodore,
Gemze de Lappe, Yuriko, Baayork Lee

The King and I (Vandamm)

A TREE GROWS IN BROOKLYN
music by Arthur Schwartz, lyrics by Dorothy Fields, book by George Abbott
& Betty Smith
opened on Broadway 4/19/51 for a run of 270 performances
selected songs: Growing Pains; He Had Refinement; I'll Buy You a Star;
I'm Like a New Broom; Look Who's Dancing; Love is the Reason; Make
the Man Love Me
cast: Shirley Booth, Johnny Johnston, Marcia Van Dyke, Moni Mitty,
Nathanial Frey, Harland Dixon, Lou Wills Jr.

PAINT YOUR WAGON
music by Frederick Loewe, lyrics & book by Alan Jay Lerner
opened on Broadway 11/12/51 for a run of 289 performances
selected songs: Another Autumn; I Still See Elsa; I Talk to the Trees; They
Call the Wind Maria; Wand'rin Star; What's Goin' on Here?
cast: James Barton, Olga San Juan, Tony Bavaar, James Mitchell, Kay Medford,
Gemze de Lappe, Marijane Maricle

1952   *Featured Song Selection:*
Wish You Were Here
from *Wish You Were Here*

Notable Musical Openings of the Year:

PAL JOEY (Revival)
music by Richard Rodgers, lyrics by Lorenz Hart, book by John O'Hara
(George Abbott uncredited)
opened on Broadway 1/3/52 for a run of 540 performances
songs: same as the original 1940 production
cast: Vivienne Segal, Harold Lang, Helen Gallagher, Lionel Stander,
Patricia Northrop, Elaine Stritch, Helen Wood, Barbara Nichols, Jack
Waldron, Robert Fortier

NEW FACES OF 1952
music, lyrics & sketches by various writers
opened on Broadway 5/16/52 for a run of 365 performances
selected songs: Boston Beguine; Guess Who I Saw Today; I'm in Love with
Miss Logan; Lizzie Bordon; Love Is a Simple Thing; Lucky Pierre; Monotonous;
Penny Candy
cast: Ronny Graham, Eartha Kitt, Robert Clary, June Carroll,
Virginia de Luce, Alice Ghostley, Carol Lawrence, Paul Lynde

WISH YOU WERE HERE
music & lyrics by Harold Rome, book by Arthur Kober & Joshua Logan
opened on Broadway 6/25/52 for a run of 598 performances
selected songs: Could Be; Don José of Far Rockaway; Flattery; Goodbye
Love; Social Director; Summer Afternoon; Tripping the Light Fantastic;
Where Did the Night Go?; Wish You Were Here
cast: Shelia Bond, Jack Cassidy, Patricia Marand, Sidney Armus,
Paul Valentine, Harry Clark, Florence Henderson, Tom Tryon, Larry Blyden,
Phyllis Newman, Reid Shelton

AN EVENING WITH BEATRICE LILLIE
music, lyrics and sketches by various writers
opened 10/2/52 for a run of 252 performances
cast: Beatrice Lillie and Reginald Gardiner

1953   *Featured Song Selection:*
Stranger in Paradise
from *Kismet*

Notable Musical Openings of the Year:

WONDERFUL TOWN
music by Leonard Bernstein, lyrics by Betty Comden & Adolph Green, book by Joseph Fields & Jerome Chodorov
opened on Broadway 2/25/53 for a run of 559 performances
selected songs: Christopher Street; Conga!; It's Love; A Little Bit in Love; Ohio; One Hundred Easy Ways; A Quiet Girl; Swing!; What a Waste; Wrong Note Rag
cast: Rosalind Russell, George Gaynes, Edie Adams, Henry Lascoe, Dort Clark, Dody Goodman, Nathaniel Frey, Joe Layton

PORGY AND BESS (Revival)
music by George Gershwin, lyrics by DuBose Heyward & Ira Gershwin, book by DuBose Heyward
opened on Broadway 3/10/53 for a run of 305 performances
songs: same as original production (1935)
cast: LeVern Hutcherson (or Leslie Scott, Irving Barnes) Leontyne Price (or Urylee Leonardos), Cab Calloway, John McCurry, Helen Colbert, Helen Thigpen, Georgia Burke, Helen Dowdy

CAN-CAN
music & lyrics by Cole Porter, book by Abe Burrows
opened on Broadway 5/7/53 for a run of 892 performances
selected songs: Allez-vous-en; Can-Can; C'est Magnifique; Come Along With Me; I Am in Love; I Love Paris; It's All Right With Me; Live and Let Live; Montmart; Never Give Anything Away; Never Never Be An Artist
cast: Lilo, Peter Cookson, Hans Conried, Gwen Verdon, Erik Rhodes, Dania Krupska, Phil Leeds, DeeDee Wood

ME AND JULIET
music by Richard Rodgers, lyrics & book Oscar Hammerstein II
opened on Broadway 5/28/53 for a run of 358 performances
selected songs: The Big Black Giant; I'm Your Girl; It's Me; Keep It Gay; Marriage-Type Love; No Other Love; A Very Special Day
cast: Isabel Bigley, Bill Hayes, Joan McCracken, Ray Walston, Mark Dawson, George S. Irving, Barbara Carroll, Shirley MacLaine

KISMET
music & lyrics by Robert Wright & George Forrest based on Alexander Borodin, book by Charles Lederer, Edwin Lester
opened on Broadway 12/3/53 for a run of 583 performances
selected songs: And This Is My Beloved; Baubles, Bangles and Beads; Night of My Nights; Not Since Nineveh; The Olive Tree; Rhymes Have I; Sands of Time; Stranger in Paradise
cast: Alfred Drake, Doretta Morrow, Joan Diener, Henry Calvin, Richard Kiley, Steve Reeves, Beatrice Kraft

1954   *Featured Song Selection:*
A Sleepin' Bee
from *House of Flowers*

Notable Musical Openings of the Year;

THE THREEPENNY OPERA
music by Kurt Weill, lyrics & book by Marc Blitzstein
opened Off-Broadway 3/10/54 for a run of 95 performances, reopened 9/20/55 for a run of 2,611 performances
selected songs: (first produced Berlin, 1928) Army Song; The Ballad of Mack the Knife; Ballad of the Easy Life; Barbara Song; Love Song; Pirate Jenny; Solomon Song; Tango-Ballad; Useless Song
cast: Lotte Lenya, Scott Merrill, Leon Lishner, Jo Sullivan, Charlotte Rae, Beatrice Arthur, Gerald Price, John Astin, Joseph Beruh, Gerrianne Raphael

THE GOLDEN APPLE
music by Jerome Moross, lyrics & book by John Latouche
opened on Broadway 3/11/54 for a run of 173 performances
selected songs: Helen Is Always Willing; It's the Going Home Together; Lazy Afternoon; My Love Is on the Way; Windflowers
cast: Priscilla Gillette, Stephen Douglass, Kaye Ballard, Jack Whiting, Bibi Osterwald, Jonathan Lucas, Portia Nelson, Jerry Stiller, Dean Michener, Shannon Bolin

BY THE BEAUTIFUL SEA
music by Arthur Schwartz, lyrics by Dorothy Fields, book by Herbert and Dorothy Fields
opened 4/8/93 for a run of 270 performances
cast: Shirley Booth, Wilbur Evans, Cameron Prud-homme, Mae Barnes, Richard France

THE PAJAMA GAME
music & lyrics by Richard Adler & Jerry Ross, book by George Abbott & Richard Bissell
opened on Broadway 5/13/54 for a run of 1,063 performances
selected songs: Hernando's Hideaway; Hey, There; I'll Never Be Jealous Again; I'm Not at All in Love; Once a Year Day; Small Talk; Steam Heat; There Once Was a Man
cast: John Raitt, Janis Paige, Eddie Foy Jr., Carol Haney, Reta Shaw, Ralph Dunn, Stanley Prager, Peter Gennaro, Shirley MacLaine

THE BOY FRIEND
music, lyrics & book by Sandy Wilson
opened on Broadway 9/30/54 for a run of 485 performances
selected songs: The Boy Friend, I Could Be Happy With You; It's Never Too Late to Fall in Love; Poor Little Pierrette; The Riviera; A Room in Bloomsbury; Sur La Plage; Won't You Charleston With Me
cast: Julie Andrews, John Hewer, Eric Berry, Ruth Altman, Bob Scheerer, Ann Wakefield, Millicent Martin, Dilys Lay, Stella Claire, Buddy Schwab

PETER PAN
music by Mark Charlap & Jule Styne, lyrics by Carolyn Leigh, Betty Comden & Adolph Green, play by James M. Barrie
opened on Broadway 10/20/54 for a run of 152 performances
selected songs: Captain Hook's Waltz; I Won't Grow Up; I'm Flying; I've Got to Crow; Mysterious Lady; Neverland; Tender Shepherd; Wendy
cast: Mary Martin, Cyril Ritchard, Kathy Nolan, Margalo Gillmore, Joe E. Marks, Sondra Lee, Joseph Stafford, Robert Harrington

FANNY
music & lyrics by Harold Rome, book by S. N. Behrman & Joshua Logan
opened on Broadway 11/4/54 for a run of 888 performances
selected songs: Be Kind to Your Parents; Fanny; I Like You; Love Is a Very Light Thing; Never Too Late for Love; Restless Heart; To My Wife; Welcome Home; Why Be Afraid to Dance?
cast: Ezio Pinza, Walter Slezak, Florence Henderson, William Tabbert, Nejla Ates, Gerald Price, Alan Carney

THE SAINT OF BLEECKER STREET
music and words by Gian Carlo Menotti
opened 12/27 54 for a run of 92 performances
cast: David Poleri, Virginia Copeland, Davis Cunningham, and Gloria Lane

HOUSE OF FLOWERS
music by Harold Arlen, lyrics by Truman Capote & Harold Arlen, book by Truman Capote
opened on Broadway 12/30/54 for a run of 165 performances
selected songs: House of Flowers; I Never Has Seen Snow; I'm Gonna Leave Off Wearin' My Shoes; A Sleepin' Bee; Smellin' of Vanilla; Two Ladies in de Shade of de Banana Tree
cast: Pearl Bailey, Diahann Carroll, Juanita Hall, Ray Walston, Dino DiLuca, Geoffrey Holder, Rawn Spearman, Frederick O'Neal, Carmen De Lavallade, Alvin Ailey, Arthur Mitchell

House of Flowers (Zinn Arthur)

1955   *Featured Song Selection:*
All of You
from *Silk Stockings*

Notable Musical Openings of the Year:

PLAIN AND FANCY
music by Albert Hague, lyrics by Arnold B. Horwitt, book by Joseph Stein & Will Glickman
opened on Broadway 1/27/55 for a run of 461 performances
selected songs: Follow Your Heart; I'll Show Him; It Wonders Me; Plenty of Pennsylvania; This Is All Very New To Me; Young and Foolish
cast: Richard Derr, Barbara Cook, David Daniels, Shirl Conway, Stefan Schnabel, Gloria Marlowe, Nancy Andrews

SILK STOCKINGS
music & lyrics by Cole Porter, book by George S. Kaufman, Leueen McGrath & Abe Burrows
opened on Broadway 2/24/55 for a run of 478 performances
selected songs: All of You; It's a Chemical Reaction, That's All; Paris Loves Lovers; The Red Blues; Satin and Silk; Silk Stockings; Too Bad; Without Love
cast: Hildegarde Neff, Don Ameche, Gretchen Wyler, George Tobias, Leon Belasco, Henry Lascoe, David Opatoshu, Julie Newmar, Onna White

DAMN YANKEES
music & lyrics by Richard Adler & Jerry Ross, book by George Abbott & Douglass Wallop (Richard Bissell uncredited)
opened on Broadway 5/5/55 for a run of 1,019 performances
selected songs: A Little Brains - a Little Talent; Heart; Near to You; Shoeless Joe from Hannibal, Mo.; Two Lost Souls; Whatever Lola Wants
cast: Gwen Verdon, Stephen Douglass, Ray Walston, Russ Brown, Shannon Bolin, Rae Allen, Jean Stapleton, Nathaniel Frey, Robert Shafer

PIPE DREAM
music by Richard Rodgers, lyrics and book by Oscar Hammerstein II
opened on Broadway 11/30/55 for a run of 246 performances
selected songs: All At Once You Love Her; The Man I Used to Be; Sweet Thursday
cast: Helen Traubel, William Johnson, Judy Tyler, Mike Kellin

1956   *Featured Song Selection:*
I've Grown Accustomed to Her Face
from *My Fair Lady*

Notable Musical Openings of the Year:

MY FAIR LADY
music by Frederick Loewe, lyrics & book by Alan Jay Lerner
opened on Broadway 3/15/56 for a run of 2,717 performances
selected songs: Get Me to the Church on Time; A Hymn to Him; I Could Have Danced All Night; I'm an Ordinary Man; I've Grown Accustomed to Her Face; On the Street Where You Live; The Rain in Spain; Show Me; Why Can't the English?; With a Little Bit of Luck; Without You; Wouldn't It Be Loverly?
cast: Rex Harrison, Julie Andrews, Stanley Holloway, Cathleen Nesbitt, Robert Coote, John Michael King, Christopher Hewett, Reid Shelton

My Fair Lady (Friedman-Abeles)

MR. WONDERFUL
music and lyrics by Jerry Bock, Larry Holofcener, and George Weiss; book by Joseph Stein and Will Glickman
opened 3/22/56 for a run of 383 performances
cast: Sammy Davis Jr., Jack Carter, Pat Marshall, Olga James, Chita Rivera

THE MOST HAPPY FELLA
music, lyrics & book by Frank Loesser
opened on Broadway 5/3/56 for a run of 676 performances
selected songs: Abbondanza; Big 'D'; Happy to Make Your Acquaintance; Joey, Joey, Joey; The Most Happy Fella; My Heart Is So Full of You; Rosabella; Somebody Somewhere; Sposalizio; Standing on the Corner; Warm All Over
cast: Robert Weede, Jo Sullivan; Art Lund, Susan Johnson, Shorty Long, Mona Paulee

LI'L ABNER
music by Gene de Paul, lyrics by Johnny Mercer, book by Norman Panama & Melvin Frank
opened on Broadway 11/15/56 for a run of 693 performances
selected songs: The Country's in the Very Best of Hands; If I Had My Druthers; Jubilation T. Cornpone; Namely You; Oh, Happy Day
cast: Edie Adams, Peter Palmer, Howard St. John, Stubby Kaye, Charlotte Rae, Tina Louise, Joe E. Marks, Julia Newmar, Grover Dale

BELLS ARE RINGING
music by Jule Styne, lyrics & book by Betty Comden & Adolph Green
opened on Broadway 11/29/56 for a run of 924 performances
selected songs: Drop That Name; Hello, Hello There!; I Met a Girl; I'm Going Back; Is It a Crime?; It's a Perfect Relationship; Just in Time; Long Before I Knew You; The Party's Over
cast: Judy Holliday, Sydney Chaplin, Jean Stapleton, Eddie Lawrence, Dort Clark, George S. Irving, Peter Gennaro, Bernie West

CANDIDE
music by Leonard Bernstein, lyrics by Richard Wilbur & various writers, book by Lillian Hellman
opened on Broadway 12/1/56 for a run of 73 performances
selected songs: The Best of All Possible Worlds; Bon Voyage; Eldorado; Glitter and Be Gay; I Am Easily Assimilated; It Must Be So; Make Our Garden Grow; Oh, Happy We; What's the Use?
cast: Max Adrian, Robert Rounseville, Barbara Cook, Irra Petina, William Olvis, Louis Edmonds, Conrad Bain

HAPPY HUNTING
music by Harold Karr, lyrics by Matt Dubey, book by Howard Lindsay and Russel Crouse
opened 12/6/56 for a run of 412 performances
cast: Ethel Merman, Fernando Lamas, Virginia Gibson, Gordon Polk

1957   *Featured Song Selection:*
Till There Was You
from *The Music Man*

Notable Musical Openings of the Year:

NEW GIRL IN TOWN
music & lyrics by Bob Merrill, book by George Abbott
opened on Broadway 5/14/57 for a run of 431 performances
selected songs: At the Check Apron Ball; Flings; If That Was Love; It's Good to Be Alive; Look at 'Er; Sunshine Girl
cast: Gwen Verdon, Thelma Ritter, George Wallace, Cameron Prud'homme, Mark Dawson

WEST SIDE STORY
music by Leonard Bernstein, lyrics by Stephen Sondheim, conception by Jerome Robbins, book by Arthur Laurents
opened on Broadway 9/26/57 for a run of 732 performances
selected songs: America; A Boy Like That; Cool; Gee, Officer Krupke; I Feel Pretty; I Have a Love; Maria; One Hand, One Heart; Something's Coming; Somewhere; Tonight
cast: Carol Lawrence, Larry Kert, Chita Rivera, Art Smith, Mickey Calin, Ken LeRoy, Lee Becker Theodore, David Winter, Tony Mordente, Eddie Roll, Martin Charnin

JAMAICA
music by Harold Arlen, lyrics by E. Y. Harburg, book by E. Y. Harburg & Fred Saidy (Joseph Stein uncredited)
opened on Broadway 10/31/57 for a run of 558 performances
selected songs: Ain't It the Truth?; Cocoanut Sweet; I Don't Think I'll End It All Today; Little Biscuit; Pity the Sunset; Pretty to Walk With; Push the Button; Take It Slow Joe
cast: Lena Horne, Rocardo Montalban, Josephine Premice, Adelaide Hall, Ossie Davis, Erik Rhodes, Joe Adams, Alvin Ailey, Billy Wilson

THE MUSIC MAN
music, book & lyrics by Meredith Wilson
opened on Broadway 12/19/57 for a run of 1,375 performances
selected songs: Gary Indiana; Goodnight My Someone; Lida Rose; Marian the Librian; My White Knight; Rock Island; The Sadder-but-Wiser Girl; Seventy-Six Trombones; Shipoopi; Sincere; Till There Was You; Trouble
cast: Robert Preston, Barbara Cook, David Burns, Pert Kelton, Iggie Wolfington, The Buffalo Bills, Eddie Hodges, Helen Raymond

1958   *Featured Song Selection:*
You Are Beautiful
from *Flower Drum Song*

Notable Musical Openings of the Year:

LA PLUME DE MA TANTE
music by Gerald Calvi, English lyrics by Ross Parker, written by Robert Dhéry
opened on Broadway 11/11/58 for a run of 835 performances
cast: Robert Dhéry, Colette Brosset, Pierre Olaf

FLOWER DRUM SONG
music by Richard Rodgers, lyrics by Oscar Hammerstein II, book by
Oscar Hammerstein & Joseph Fields
opened on Broadway 12/1/58 for a run of 600 performances
selected songs: Don't Marry Me; Grant Avenue; A Hundred Million
Miracles; I Am Going to Like It Here; I Enjoy Being a Girl; Love, Look
Away; Sunday; You Are Beautiful
cast: Miyoshi Umeki, Larry Blyden, Pat Suzuki, Juanita Hall, Ed Kenney,
Keye Luke, Arabella Hong, Jack Soo, Anita Ellis

1959   *Featured Song Selection:*
Everything's Coming Up Roses
from *Gypsy*

Notable Musical Openings of the Year;

REDHEAD
music by Albert Hague, lyrics by Dorothy Fields, book by Herbert &
Dorothy Fields, Sidney Sheldon & David Shaw
opened on Broadway 2/5/59 for a run of 452 performances
selected songs: Erbie Fitch's Twitch; Just for Once; Look Who's In Love;
Merely Marvelous; My Girl Is Just Enough Woman for Me; The Right
Finger of My Left Hand; The Uncle Sam Rag
cast: Gwen Verdon, Richard Kiley, Leonard Stone, Doris Rich,
Cynthia Latham

DESTRY RIDES AGAIN
music & lyrics by Harold Rome, book by Leonard Gershe
opened on Broadway 4/23/59 for a run of 473 performances
selected songs: Anyone Would Love You; Ballad of the Gun; I Know Your
Kind; I Say Hello; Once Knew a Fella; That Ring on the Finger
cast: Andy Griffith, Dolores Gray, Scott Brady, Jack Prince, Swen Swenson,
Marc Breaux, George Reeder

ONCE UPON A MATTRESS
music by Mary Rodgers, lyrics by Marshall Barer, book by Jay Thompson,
Dean Fuller & Marshall Barer
opened on Broadway 5/11/59 for a run of 460 performances
selected songs: Happily Ever After; In a Little While; Many Moons Ago;
Sensitivity; Shy; Very Soft Shoes
cast: Joseph Bova, Carol Burnett, Allen Case, Jack Gilford, Anne Jones,
Matt Mattox, Harry Snow, Jane White

GYPSY
music by Jule Styne, lyrics by Stephen Sondheim, book by Arthur Laurents
opened on Broadway 5/21/59 for a run of 702 performances
selected songs: All I Need Is the Girl; Everything's Coming Up Roses; If
Momma Was Married; Let Me Entertain You; Little Lamb;
Rose's Turn; Small World; Some People; Together; You Gotta Have a
Gimmick; You'll Never Get Away from Me
cast: Ethel Merman, Jack Klugman, Sandra Church, Lane Bradbury,
Maria Karnilova, Paul Wallace, Jacqueline Mayro, Karen Moore, Joe Silver

Gypsy (Friedman-Abeles)

TAKE ME ALONG
music & lyrics by Bob Merrill, book by Joseph Stein & Robert Russell
opened on Broadway 10/22/59 for a run of 448 performances
selected songs: But Yours; I Get Embarrassed; I Would Die; Nine O'Clock;
Promise Me a Rose; Sid Ol' Kid; Staying Young; Take Me Along; We're
Home
cast: Jackie Gleason, Walter Pidgeon, Eileen Herlie, Robert Morse,
Una Merkel, Peter Conlow, Susan Luckey, Valerie Harper

THE SOUND OF MUSIC
music by Richard Rodgers, lyrics by Oscar Hammerstein II, book by
Howard Lindsay & Russell Crouse
opened on Broadway 11/16/59 for a run of 1,443 performances
selected songs: An Ordinary Couple; Climb Ev'ry Mountain; Do-Re-Mi;
Edelweiss; How Can Love Survive?; The Lonely Goatherd; Maria; My
Favorite Things; Sixteen Going on Seventeen; So Long, Farewell; The
Sound of Music
cast: Mary Martin, Theodore Bikel, Patricia Neway, Kurt Kasznar,
Marion Marlowe, Lauri Peters, Brian Davies, John Randolph, Nan McFarland,
Joey Heatherton

LITTLE MARY SUNSHINE
music, lyrics & book by Rick Besoyan
opened Off-Broadway 11/18/59 for a run of 1,143 performances
selected songs: Colorado Love Call; Do You Ever Dream of Vienna?; Every
Little Nothing; Look for a Sky of Blue; Naughty, Naughty Nancy; Once in a
Blue Moon; Tell a Handsome Stranger
cast: Eileen Brennan, William Graham, John McMartin, Elmarie Wendel

FIORELLO!
music by Jerry Bock, lyrics by Sheldon Harnick, book by Jerome Weidman
& George Abbott
opened on Broadway 11/23/59 for a run of 795 performances
selected songs: I Love a Cop; Little Tin Box; The Name's LaGuardia;
Politics and Poker; Till Tomorrow; When Did I Fall in Love?
cast: Tom Bosley, Patricia Wilson, Ellen Hanley, Howard Da Silva,
Mark Dawson, Nathaniel Frey, Pat Stanley, Eileen Rodgers, Ron Husmann

1960   *Featured Song Selection:*
Camelot
from *Camelot*

Notable Musical Openings of the Year:

BYE BYE BIRDIE
music by Charles Strouse, lyrics by Lee Adams, book by Michael Stewart
opened on Broadway 4/14/60 for a run of 607 performances
selected songs; An English Teacher; Baby, Talk to Me; How Lovely to Be a
Woman; Kids; A Lot of Livin' to Do; One Boy; One Last Kiss; Put on a
Happy Face; Rosie; The Telephone Hour
cast: Chita Rivera, Dick Van Dyke, Kay Medford, Paul Lynde, Dick Gautier,
Michael J. Pollard, Susan Watson, Charles Nelson Reilly

THE FANTASTICKS
music by Harvey Schmidt, lyrics & book by Tom Jones
opened Off-Broadway 5/3/60 (still running 12/1/93)
selected songs: I Can See It; It Depends on What You Pay; Much More;
Plant a Radish; Round and Round; Soon It's Gonna Rain; They Were You;
Try to Remember
cast: Jerry Orbach, Rita Gardner, Kenneth Nelson, William Larson,
Hugh Thomas, Tom Jones, George Curley, Richard Stauffer

IRMA LA DOUCE
music by Marguerite Monnot, lyrics & book by Julian Moore, David Heneker
& Monty Norman
opened on Broadway 9/29/60 for a run of 524 performances
selected songs: The Bridge of Caulaincourt; Dis-Donc; Irma la Douce; Our
Language of Love; There Is Only One Paris for That
cast: Elizabeth Seal, Keith Mitchell, Clive Revill, George S. Irving,
Stuart Damon, Fred Gwynne, Elliott Gould

TENDERLOIN
music by Jerry Bock, lyrics by Sheldon Harnick, book by George Abbott and
Jerome Weidman
opened 10/17/60 for a run of 216 performances
cast: Maurice Evans, Ron Husmann, Wynne Miller, Eileen Rodgers

THE UNSINKABLE MOLLY BROWN
music & lyrics by Meredith Wilson, book by Richard Morris
opened on Broadway 11/3/60 for a run of 532 performances
selected songs: Are You Sure?; Belly Up to the Bar, Boys; Colorado, My Home;
Dolce Far Niente; I Ain't Down Yet; I'll Never Say No to You; My Own
Brass Bed
cast: Tammy Grimes, Harve Presnell, Cameron Prud'homme, Mony Dalmes,
Edith Meiser, Mitchell Gregg, Christopher Hewett

CAMELOT
music by Frederick Loewe, lyrics & book by Alan Jay Lerner
opened on Broadway 12/3/60 for a run of 873 performances
selected songs: Before I Gaze at You Again; Camelot; C'est Moi; Fie on
Goodness; Follow Me; Guenevere; How to Handle a Woman; I Loved You
Once in Silence; I Wonder What the King is Doing Tonight; If Ever I Would
Leave You; The Lusty Month of May; The Simple Joys of Maidenhood;
Then You May Take Me to the Fair; What Do the Simple Folk Do?
cast: Richard Burton, Julie Andrews, Roddy McDowall, Robert Coote,
Robert Goulet, M'el Dowd, John Cullum, Bruce Yarnell, David Hurst,
Michael Kermoyan

Camelot (Friedman-Abeles)

WILDCAT
music by Cy Coleman, lyrics by Carolyn Leigh, book by N. Richard Nash
opened 12/16/60 for a run of 171 performances
selected songs: Hey, Look Me Over
cast: Lucille Ball, Keith Andes, Edith King, Paula Stewart

DO RE MI
music by Jule Styne, lyrics by Betty Comden & Adolph Green, book by
Garson Kanin
opened on Broadway 12/26/60 for a run of 400 performances
selected songs: Adventure; Cry Like the Wind; Fireworks; I Know About
Love; It's Legitimate; The Late Late Show; Make Someone Happy; What's
New at the Zoo?
cast: Phil Silvers, Nancy Walker, John Reardon, David Burns, George Matthews,
George Givot, Nancy Dussault

1961   *Featured Song Selection:*
I Believe in You
from *How to Succeed in Business Without Really Trying*

Notable Musical Openings of the Year:

CARNIVAL
music & lyrics by Bob Merrill, book by Michael Stewart
opened on Broadway 4/13/61 for a run of 719 performances
selected songs: Always Always You; Beautiful Candy; Direct from Vienna;
Grand Imperial Cirque de Paris; Love Makes the World Go Round; Mira;
She's My Love; Yes, My Heart
cast: Anna Maria Alberghetti, James Mitchell, Kaye Ballard, Pierre Olaf,
Jerry Orbach, Henry Lascoe, Anita Gillette

MILK AND HONEY
music & lyrics by Jerry Herman, book by Don Appell
opened on Broadway 10/10/61 for a run of 543 performances
selected songs: As Simple As That; Let's Not Waste a Moment; Like A
Young Man; Milk and Honey; Shalom; That Was Yesterday; There's No
Reason in the World;
cast: Robert Weede, Mimi Benzell, Molly Picon, Tommy Rall, Lanna Saunders,
Juki Arkin

HOW TO SUCCEED IN BUSINESS WITHOUT REALLY TRYING
music & lyrics by Frank Loesser, book by Abe Burrows
opened on Broadway 10/14/61 for a run of 1,417 performances
selected songs: Brotherhood of Man; Coffee Break; The Company Way;
Grand Old Ivy; I Believe in You; Paris Original; Rosemary; A Secretary Is
Not a Toy
cast: Robert Morse, Rudy Vallee, Bonnie Scott, Virginia Martin,
Charles Nelson Reilly, Ruth Kobart, Sammy Smith, Donna McKechnie

SUBWAYS ARE FOR SLEEPING
music by Jule Styne, lyrics and book by Betty Comden and Adolph Green
opened on Broadway 12/27/61 for a run of 205 performances
cast: Sydney Chaplin, Carol Lawrence, Orson Bean, Phyllis Newman

1962   *Featured Song Selection:*
Comedy Tonight
from *A Funny Thing Happened On the Way To the Forum*

Notable Musical Openings of the Year:

NO STRINGS
music & lyrics by Richard Rodgers, book by Samuel Taylor
opened on Broadway 3/15/62 for a run of 580 performances
selected songs: La La La; Loads of Love; Look No Further; Maine; Nobody
Told Me; No Strings; The Sweetest Sounds
cast: Richard Kiley, Diahann Carroll, Polly Rowles, Noelle Adam,
Bernice Massi, Don Chastain, Alvin Epstein, Mitchell Gregg

I CAN GET IT FOR YOU WHOLESALE
music & lyrics by Harold Rome, book by Jerome Weidman
opened on Broadway 3/22/62 for a run of 300 performances
selected songs: Miss Marmelstein; Who Knows
cast: Elliott Gould, Sheree North, Lillian Roth, Harold Lang, Marilyn Cooper,
Barbra Streisand, Bambi Linn

A FUNNY THING HAPPENED ON THE WAY TO THE FORUM
music & lyrics by Stephen Sondheim, book by Burt Shevelove & Larry Gelbart
opened on Broadway 5/8/62 for a run of 964 performances
selected songs: Bring Me My Bride; Comedy Tonight; Everybody Ought to
Have a Maid; Free; I'm Calm; Impossible; Love I Hear; Lovely; Pretty Little
Picture; That'll Show Him
cast: Zero Mostel, John Carradine, Raymond Walburn, Jack Gilford,
David Burns, Ruth Kobart, Brian Davies, Preshy Marker, Ronald Holgate,
Eddie Phillips

STOP THE WORLD—I WANT TO GET OFF
music, lyrics & book by Leslie Bricusse & Anthony Newley
opened on Broadway 10/3/62 for a run of 555 performances
selected songs: Gonna Build a Mountain; Once in a Lifetime; Someone Nice
Like You; Typically English; What Kind Of Fool Am I?
cast: Anthony Newley, Anna Quayle, Jennifer Baker, Susan Baker

MR. PRESIDENT
music & lyrics by Irving Berlin, book by Howard Lindway and Russell Crouse
opened on Broadway 10/20/62 for a run of 265 performances
selected songs: Is He the Only Man in the World?; They Love Me; Pigtails
and Freckles
cast: Robert Ryan, Nanette Fabray, Anita Gillette

LITTLE ME
music by Cy Coleman, lyrics by Carolyn Leigh, book by Neil Simon
opened on Broadway 11/17/62 for a run of 257 performances
selected songs: Be a Performer; Boom Boom; Here's to Us; I Love You;
I've Got Your Number; The Other Side of the Tracks; Poor Little Hollywood
Star; Real Live Girl
cast: Sid Ceasar, Virginia Martin, Nancy Andrews, Mort Marshall, Joey Faye,
Swen Swenson, Peter Turgeon, Mickey Deems, Gretchen Cryer

1963   *Featured Song Selection:*
Where Is Love?
from *Oliver!*

Notable Musical Openings of the Year:

OLIVER!
music, lyrics & book by Lionel Bart
opened on Broadway 1/6/63 for a run of 774 performances
selected songs: As Long As He Needs Me; Consider Yourself; Food
Glorious Food; I'd Do Anything; It's a Fine Life; Oom-Pah-Pah; Reviewing
the Situation; Where Is Love?; Who Will Buy?; You've Got to Pick a Pocket
or Two
cast: Clive Revill, Georgia Brown, Bruce Prochnik, Willoughby Goddard,
Hope Jackman, Danny Sewell, David Jones, Geoffrey Lamb

TOVARICH
music by Lee Pockriss, lyrics by Anne Croswell, book by David Shaw
opened on Broadway 3/18/63 for a run of 264 performances
cast: Vivien Leigh, Jean Pierre Aumont, Alexander Scourby, Louise Troy,
George S. Irving

SHE LOVES ME
music by Jerry Bock, lyrics by Sheldon Harnick, book by Joe Masteroff
opened on Broadway 4/23/63 for a run of 301 performances
selected songs: Dear Friend; Days Gone By; Grand Knowing You; Ice Cream; She Loves Me; Tonight at Eight; A Trip to the Library; Twelve Days to Christmas; Will He Like Me?
cast: Barbara Cook, Daniel Massey, Barbara Baxley, Jack Cassidy, Ludwig Donath, Nathaniel Frey, Ralph Williams

HERE'S LOVE
music, book & lyrics by Meredith Willson
opened on Broadway 10/3/63 for a run of 338 performances
cast: Janis Paige, Craig Stevens, Laurence Naismith, Fred Gwynne, Valerie Lee

110 IN THE SHADE
music by Harvey Schmidt, lyrics by Tom Jones, book by N. Richard Nash
opened on Broadway 10/24/63 for a run of 330 performances
selected songs: Everything Beautiful Happens at Night; Is It Really Me?; Little Red Hat; Love, Don't Turn Away; Melisande; Old Maid; Rain Song; Simple Little Things; You're Not Foolin' Me
cast: Robert Horton, Inga Swenson, Stephen Douglass, Will Geer, Steve Roland, Anthony Teague, Lesley Ann Warren, Gretchen Cryer

1964

Featured Song Selection:
Hello, Dolly!
from *Hello, Dolly!*

Notable Musical Openings of the Year:

HELLO, DOLLY!
music & lyrics by Jerry Herman, book by Michael Stewart
opened on Broadway 1/16/64 for a run of 2,844 performances
selected songs: Before the Parade Passes By; Dancing; Hello, Dolly!; It Only Takes a Moment; It Takes a Woman; Put on Your Sunday Clothes; Ribbons Down My Back; So Long, Dearie
cast: Carol Channing, David Burns, Eileen Brennan, Sondra Lee, Charles Nelson Reilly, Jerry Dodge, Gordon Connell, Igors Gavon, Alice Playton, David Hartman

Hello, Dolly!

WHAT MAKES SAMMY RUN?
music & lyrics by Ervin Drake, book by Budd & Stuart Schulberg
opened on Broadway 2/27/64 for a run of 540 performances
selected songs: The Friendliest Thing; My Home Town; A Room Without Windows; Something to Live For; A Tender Spot
cast: Steve Lawrence, Sally Ann Howes, Robert Alda, Bernice Massi, Barry Newman, Walter Klavun

FUNNY GIRL
music by Jule Styne, lyrics by Bob Merrill, book by Isobel Lennart
opened on Broadway 3/26/64 for a run of 1,348 performances
selected songs: Cornet Man; Don't Rain on My Parade; I Want to Be Seen With You Tonight; I'm the Greatest Star; The Music That Makes Me Dance; People; Sadie, Sadie; Who Are You Now?; You Are Woman
cast: Barbara Streisand; Sydney Chaplin, Kay Medford, Danny Meehan, Jean Stapleton, Roger DeKoven, Joseph Macaulay, Lainie Kazan; Buzz Miller, George Reeder, Larry Fuller

ANYONE CAN WHISTLE
music & lyrics by Stephen Sondheim, book by Arthur Laurents
opened on Broadway 4/4/64 for a run of 9 performances
selected songs: Anyone Can Whistle, I've Got You to Lean On, There Won't Be Trumpets (cut)
cast: Angela Lansbury, Lee Remick, Harry Guardino, Gabriel Dell

HIGH SPIRITS
music, lyrics & book by Hugh Martin & Timothy Gray
opened on Broadway 4/7/64 for a run of 375 performances
selected songs: The Bicycle Song; Faster Than Sound; Forever and a Day; Home Sweet Heaven; I Know Your Heart; If I Gave You; Something Is Coming to Tea; Was She Prettier Than I?
cast: Beatrice Lillie, Tammy Grimes, Edward Woodward, Louise Troy

FIDDLER ON THE ROOF
music by Jerry Bock, lyrics by Sheldon Harnick, book by Joseph Stein
opened on Broadway 9/22/64 for a run of 3,242 performances
selected songs: Anatevka; Do You Love Me?; Far from the Home I Love; If I Were a Rich Man; Matchmaker, Matchmaker; Miracle of Miracles; Now I Have Everything; Sabbath Prayer; Sunrise, Sunset; To Life; Tradition
cast: Sero Mostel, Maria Karnilova, Beatrice Arthur, Joanna Merlin, Austin Pendleton, Bery Convy, Julia Migenes, Michael Granger, Tanya Everett, Leonard Frey, Maurice Edwards

GOLDEN BOY
music by Charles Strouse, lyrics by Lee Adams, book by Clifford Odets & William Gibson
opened on Broadway 10/20/64 for a run of 569 performances
selected songs: Don't Forget 127th Street; I Want to Be With You; Lorna's Here; Night Song; This Is the Life; While the City Sleeps
cast: Sammy Davis Jr., Billy Daniels, Paula Wayne, Kenneth Tobey, Ted Beniades, Louis Gossett, Jaime Rogers, Lola Falana

1965

Featured Song Selection:
The Impossible Dream
from *Man of La Mancha*

Notable Musical Openings of the Year:

DO I HEAR A WALTZ?
music by Richard Rodgers, lyrics by Stephen Sondheim, book by Arthur Laurents
opened on Broadway 3/18/65 for a run of 220 performances
selected songs: Do I Hear a Waltz?; Here We Are Again; Moon in My Window; Someone Like You; Someone Woke Up; Stay; Take the Moment; Thank You So Much; This Week Americans; We're Gonna Be Alright; What Do We Do? We Fly!
cast: Elizabeth Allen, Sergio Franchi, Carol Bruce, Madeline Sherwood, Julienne Marie, Stuart Damon, Fleury D'Antonakis, Jack Manning

HALF A SIXPENCE
music & lyrics by David Heneker, book by Beverly Cross
opened on Broadway 4/25/65 for a run of 512 performances
selected songs: Flash Bang Wallop; Half a Sixpence; If the Rain's Got to Fall; Long Ago; Money to Burn; She's Too Far Above Me
cast: Tommy Steele, Ann Shoemaker, James Grout, Carrie Nye, Polly James, Grover Dale, Will McKenzie, John Cleese

THE ROAR OF THE GREASEPAINT—THE SMELL OF THE CROWD
music, lyrics & book by Nancy Bricusse & anthony Newley
opened on Broadway 5/16/65 for a run of 232 performances
selected songs: Feeling Good; The Joker; Look at That Face; My First Love Song; My Way; Nothing Can Stop Me Now; Sweet Beginning; Where Would You Be Without Me?; Who Can I Turn To?; A Wonderful Day Like Today
cast: Anthony Newley, Cyril Ritchard, Sally Smith, Gilbert Price, Joyce Jillson

ON A CLEAR DAY YOU CAN SEE FOREVER
music by Burton Lane, lyrics & book by Alan Jay Lerner
opened on Broadway 10/17/65 for a run of 280 performances
selected songs: Come Back to Me; Hurry! It's Lonely Up Here; Melinda; On a Clear Day; On the S. S. Bernard Cohn; She Wasn't You; Wait Till We're Sixty-Five; What Did I Have That I Don't Have?
cast: Barbara Harris, John Cullum, Titos Vandis, William Daniels, Clifford David, Rae Allen

MAN OF LA MANCHA
music by Mitch Leigh, lyrics by Joe Darion, book by Dale Wasserman
opened Off Broadway 11/22/65, moved to Broadway 3/68 for a total run of 2,328 performances
selected songs: Dulcinea; I Really Like Him; The Impossible Dream; Knight of the Woeful Countenance; Little Bird, Little Bird; Man of La Mancha; To Each His Dulcinea
cast: Richard Kiley, Joan Diener, Irving Jacobson, Ray Middleton, Robert Rounseville, Jon Cypher, Gerrianne Raphael

1966

Featured Song Selection:
Cabaret
from *Cabaret*

Notable Musical Openings of the Year:

SWEET CHARITY
music by Cy Coleman, lyrics by Dorothy Fields, book by Neil Simon
opened on Broadway 1/29/66 for a run of 608 performances
selected songs: Baby Dream Your Dreams; Big Spender; If My Friends Could See Me Now; I'm a Brass Band; The Rhythm of Life; Sweet Charity; There's Gotta Be Something Better Than This; Where Am I Going?
Gwen Verdon, John McMartin, Helen Gallagher, Thelma Oliver, James Luisi, Ruth Buzzi, Barbara Sharma

MAME
music & lyrics by Jerry Herman, book by Jerome Lawrence & Robert E. Lee
opened on Broadway 5/24/66 for a run of 1,508 performances
selected songs: Bosom Buddies; If He Walked Into My Life; It's Today; Mame; My Best Girl; Open a New Window; That's How Young I Feel; We Need a Little Christmas
cast: Angela Lansbury, Beatrice Arthur, Jane Connell, Willard Waterman, Frankie michaels, Charles Braswell, Jerry Lanning

THE APPLE TREE
music by Jerry Bock, lyrics by Sheldon Harnick, book by Jerry Bock & Sheldon Harnick, with Jerome Coopersmith
opened on Broadway 10/18/66 for a run of 463 performances
selected songs: Beautiful, Beautiful World; Eve; Go to Sleep, Whatever You Are; Gorgeous; Here in Eden; It's a Fish; Oh, to Be a Movie Star; What Makes Me Love Him
cast: Barbara Harris, Larry Blyden, Alan Alda, Carmen Alvarez, Robert Klein

CABARET
music by John Kander, lyrics by Fred Ebb, book by Joe Masteroff
opened on Broadway 11/20/66 for a run of 1,165 performances
selected songs: Cabaret; Don't Tell Mama; If You Could See Her; It Couldn't Please Me More; Married; The Money Song; Perfectly Marvelous; Tomorrow Belongs to Me; Two Ladies; Willkommen
cast: Jill Haworth, Jack Gilford, Bert Convy, Lotte Lenya, Joel Grey, Peg Murray, Edward Winter

Cabaret

I DO! I DO!
music by Harvey Schmidt, lyrics & book by Tom Jones
opened on Broadway 12/5/66 for a run of 560 performances
selected songs: The Honeymoon Is Over; I Love My Wife; Love Isn't Everything; My Cup Runneth Over; Nobody's Perfect; Roll Up the Ribbons; Someone Needs Me; When the Kids Get Married; Where Are the Snows?
cast: Mary Martin, Robert Preston

1967   *Featured Song Selection:*
Maman
from *Mata Hari*

Notable Musical Openings of the Year:

MATA HARI
music by Edward Thomas, lyrics by Martin Charnin, book by Jerome Coopersmith
Note: The show closed out of town, and never opened on Broadway.
cast: Blythe Danner, Mark Dempsey, Marisa Mell, Pernell Roberts, Martha Schlamme
(1967 was not a great Broadway year for new musicals, partly because it was so difficult to compete with several very long runs of shows that had opened in previous seasons but were still big hits. This interesting song from one of the most notable disasters in Broadway history seemed an interesting choice to represent the year.)

YOU'RE A GOOD MAN, CHARLIE BROWN
music, lyrics & book by Clark Gesner
opened Off-Broadway 3/7/67 for a run of 1,597 performances
selected songs: Book Report; Happiness; The Kite; Little Known Facts; My Blanket and Me; Suppertime; T.E.A.M. (The Baseball Game); You're a Good Man, Charlie Brown
cast: Bill Hinnant, Reva Rose, Karen Johnson, Bob Balaban, Skip Hinnant, Gary Burghoff

1968   *Featured Song Selection:*
Promises, Promises
from *Promises, Promises*

Notable Musical Openings of the Year:

YOUR OWN THING
music & lyrics by Hal Hester & Danny Apolinar, book by Donald Driver
opened on Broadway 1/13/68 for a run of 933 performances
selected songs: Come Away Death; The Flowers; I'm Me!; I'm on My Way to the Top; The Middle Years; The Now Generation
cast: Leland Palmer, Marian Mercer, Rusty Thacker, Tom Liggon, Danny Apolinar, Michael Valenti, John Kuhner

THE HAPPY TIME
music by John Kander, lyrics by Fred Ebb, book by N. Richard Nash
opened on Broadway 1/18/68 for a run of 286 performances
selected songs: A Certain Girl; The Happy Time; I Don't Remember You; The Life of the Party; Please Stay; Seeing Things: Tomorrow Morning
cast: Robert Goulet, David Wayne, Mike Rupert, Julie Gregg, George S. Irving, Charles Durning

GEORGE M!
music & lyrics by George M. Cohan, book by Michael Stewart, John & Fran Pascal
opened on Broadway 4/10/68 for a run of 427 performances
selected songs: All Aboard for Broadway; Billie; Forty-Five Minutes from Broadway; Give My Regards to Broadway; Harrigan; Mary's a Grand Old Name; Musical Comedy Man; My Town; Nellie Kelly, I Love You; Over There;Ring to the Name of the Rose; So Long, Mary; Yankee Doodle Dandy; You're a Grand Old Flag
cast: Joel Grey, Betty Ann Grove, Jerry Dodge, Jill O'Hara, Bernadette Peters, Jamie Donnelly, Jacqueline Alloway, Loni Ackerman

HAIR
music by Galt MacDermot, lyrics & book by Gerome Ragni & James Rado
opened on Broadway 4/29/68 for a run of 1,750 performances
selected songs: Ain't Got No; Aquarius; Easy to Be Hard; Frank Mills; Good Morning Starshine; Hair; Hare Krishna; I Got Life; Let the Sunshine In; Manchester England; Where Do I Go?
cast: Steve Curry, Ronald Dyson, Sally Eaton, Leata Galloway, Paul Jabara, Diane Keaton, Lynn Kellogg, Melba Moore, Shelley Plimpton, James Rado, Gerome Ragni, Lamont Washington

ZORBA
music by John Kander, lyrics by Fred Ebb, book by Joseph Stein
opened on Broadway 11/17/68 for a run of 305 performances
selected songs: The Butterfly; The First Time; Happy Birthday; I Am Free; Life Is; No Boom Boom; Only Love; The Top of the Hill; Y'assou
cast: Herschel Bernardi, Maria Karnilova, John Cunningham, Carmen Alvarez, Lorraine Serabian, James Luisi

PROMISES, PROMISES
music by Burt Bacharach, lyrics by Hal David, book by Neil Simon
opened on Broadway 12/1/68 for a run of 1,281 performances
selected songs: I'll Never Fall in Love Again; Knowing When to Leave; Promises, Promises; She Likes Basketball; Wanting Things; Whoever You Are; You'll Think of Someone; A Young Pretty Girl Like You
cast: Jarry Orbach, Jill O'Hara, Edward Winter, Norman Shelly, A. Larry Haines, Marian Mercer, Ken Howard, Donna McKechnie

DAMES AT SEA
music by Jim Wise, lyrics & book by George Haimsohn & Jack Millstein
opened on Broadway 12/20/68 for a run of 575 performances
selected songs: Choo-Choo Honeymoon; Dames at Sea; Good Times Are Here to Stay; It's You; That Mister of Mine; Raining in My Heart; The Sailor of My Dreams; Singapore Sue; Star Tar
cast: Bernadette Peters, David Christmas, Steve Elmore, Tamara Long

1969   *Featured Song Selection:*
Somebody
from *Celebration*

Notable Musical Openings of the Year:

CELEBRATION
music by Harvey Schmidt, lyrics & book by Tom Jones
opened Off-Broadway 1/22/69 for a run of 109 performances
selected songs: Celebration; Fifty Million Years Ago; Love Song; Mr. Somebody in the Sky; My Garden; Somebody; Where Did It Go?
cast: Michael Glenn-Smith, Susan Watson, The Revelers

COCO
music by André Previn, lyrics & book by Alan Jay Lerner
opened on Broadway 12/18/69
selected songs: Fiasco; Let's Go Home; Ohrbach's, Bloomingdale's, Best and Saks'; When Your Lover Says Goodbye; A Woman Is How She Loves
cast: Katharine Hepburn, George Rose, Gale Dixon, David Holliday

1970   *Featured Song Selection:*
Being Alive
from *Company*

Notable Musical Openings of the Year:

PURLIE
music by Gary Geld, lyrics by Peter Udell, book by Ossie Davis, Philip Rose & Peter Udell
opened on Broadway 3/15/70 for a run of 688 performances
selected songs: First Thing Monday Mornin'; I Got Love; New Fangled Preacher Man; Purlie; Skinn'a Cat; Walk Him Up the Stairs
cast: Cleavon Little, Melba Moore, John Heffernan, Sherman Helmsley, Novella Nelson; George Faison

APPLAUSE
music by Charles Strouse, lyrics by Lee Adams, book by Betty Comden & Adolph Green
opened on Broadway 3/30/70 for a run of 896 performances
selected songs: Applause; But Alive; Fasten Your Seat Belts; One of a Kind; Something Greater; Think How It's Gonna Be; Welcome to the Theatre; Who's That Girl?
cast: Lauren Bacall, Len Cariou, Robert Mandan, Ann Williams, Brandon Maggart, Penny Fuller, Lee Roy Reams, Bonnie Franklin

COMPANY
music & lyrics by Stephen Sondheim, book by George Furth
opened on Broadway 4/26/70 for a run of 706 performances
selected songs: Another Hundred People; Barcelona; Being Alive; Company; Getting Married Today; The Ladies Who Lunch; The Little Things You Do Together; Someone Is Waiting; Sorry-Grateful; What Would We Do Without You?; You Could Drive a Person Crazy
cast: Dean Jones, Elaine Stritch; Barbara Barrie, John Cunningham, Charles Kimbrough, Donna McKechnie, Charles Braswell, Susan Browing, Steve Elmore, Beth Howland, Pamela Myers, Merle Louise

THE ROTHSCHILDS
music by Jerry Bock, lyrics by Sheldon Harnick, book by Sherman Yellen
opened on Broadway 10/19/70 for a run of 507 performances
selected songs: He Tossed a Coin; I'm in Love! I'm in Love!; In My Own Lifetime; One Room; Rothschild and Sons; Sons
cast: Hal Linden, Paul Hecht, Leila Martin, Keene Curtis, Jill Clayburgh, Chris Sarandon

1971   *Featured Song Selection:*
Broadway Baby
from *Follies*

Notable Musical Openings of the Year:

NO, NO, NANETTE (Revival)
music by Vincent Youmans, lyrics by Irving Ceasar, book by Burt Shevelove
opened on Broadway 1/19/71 for a run of 861 performances
songs same as 1925 production plus; I've Confessed to the Breeze; Take a Little One-Step
cast: Ruby Keeler, Jack Gilford, Bobby Van, Helen Gallagher, Patsy Kelly, Susan Watson, Roger Rathburn, Loni Ackerman

FOLLIES
music & lyrics by Stephen Sondheim, book by James Goldman
opened on Broadway 4/4/71 for a run of 522 performances
selected songs: Ah, Paris; Broadway Baby; Could I Leave You?; I'm Still Here; In Buddy's Eyes; Losing My Mind; The Right Girl; The Road You Didn't Take; The Story of Lucy and Jessie; Too Many Mornings; Waiting for the Girls Upstairs; Who's That Woman?
cast: Alexis Smith, Gene Nelson, Dorothy Collins, John McMartin, Yvonne DeCarlo, Fifi D'Orsay, Mary McMarty, Ethel Shutta, Arnold Moss, Ethel Barrymore Colt, Michael Bartlett, Sheila Smith, Justine Johnston, Virginia Sandifur, Kurt Peterson, Victoria Mallory, Marti Rolph

GODSPELL
music & lyrics by Stephen Schwartz, book by John-Michael Tebelak
opened Off-Broadway 5/17/71; moved to Broadway 6/22/76 for a total of 2,651 performances
selected songs: All for the Best; All Good Gifts; Day by Day; Light of the World; On the Willows; Prepare Ye the Way of the Lord; Save the People; Turn Back, O Man; We Beseech Thee
cast: Lamar Alford, David Haskell, Johanne Jonas, Robin Lamont, Sonia Manzano, Jeffrey Mylett, Stephen Nathan

JESUS CHRIST SUPERSTAR
music by Andrew Lloyd Webber, lyrics by Tim Rice, conception by Tom O'Horgan
opened on Broadway 10/12/71 for a run of 720 performances
selected songs: Could We Start Again, Please?; Everything's Alright; Heaven on Their Minds; I Don't Know How to Love Him; King Herod's Song; Superstar; What's the Buzz?
cast: Jeff Fenholt, Yvonne Elliman, Ben Vereen, Barry Dennen, Anita Morris

TWO GENTLEMEN OF VERONA
music by Galt MacDermot, lyrics by John Guare, book by John Guare & Mel Shapiro
opened on Broadway 12/1/71 for a run of 627 performances
selected songs: Bring All the Boys Back Home; Calla Lily Lady; Follow the Rainbow; Night Letter; Who Is Sylvia?
cast: Jonelle Allen, Diana Davila, Clifton Davis, Raul Julia, Norman Matlock, Alix Elias, John Bottoms, Stockard Channing

1972   *Featured Song Selection:*
Summer Nights
from *Grease*

Notable Musical Openings of the Year:

GREASE
music, lyrics & book by Jim Jacobs & Warren Casey
opened off Broadway, later moved to Broadway for a total of 3,388 performances
selected songs: Alone at a Drive-in Movie; Beauty School Dropout; Freddy, My Love; Greased Lightnin'; It's Raining on Prom Night; Look at Me, I'm Sandra Dee; Mooning; Summer Nights; There Are Worse Things I Could Do; We Go Together
cast: Adrienne Barbeau, Barry Bostwick, Carole Demas, Timothy Meyers

SUGAR
music by Jule Styne, lyrics by Bob Merrill, book by Peter Stone
opened on Broadway 4/09/72 for a run of 505 performances
selected songs: Sugar; Sun on My Face; What Do You Give to a Man Who's Had Everything; When You Meet a Man in Chicago
cast: Robert Morse, Tony Roberts, Cyril Ritchard, Elaine Joyce, Sheila Smith, Steve Condos, Pamela Blair

DON'T BOTHER ME, I CAN'T COPE
music & lyrics by Micki Grant, conception by Vinnette Carroll
opened on Broadway 4/19/72 for a run of 1,065 performances
selected songs: Don't Bother Me, I Can't Cope; Fighting for Pharaoh; Good Vibrations; It Takes a Whole Lot of Human Feeling; Thank Heaven for You
cast: Alex Bradford, Hope Clarke, Micki Grant, Bobby Hill, Arnold Wilkerson

PIPPIN
music & lyrics by Stephen Schwartz, book by Roger O. Hirson (Bob Fosse uncredited)
opened on Broadway 10/23/72 for a run of 1,944 performances
selected songs: Corner of the Sky; Extraordinary; Kind of Woman; Love Song; Magic to Do; Morning Glow; No Time at All; On the Right Track; Simple Joys
cast: Eric Berry, Jill Clayburgh, Leland Palmer, Irene Ryan, Ben Vereen, John Rubenstein, Ann Reinking

1973   *Featured Song Selection:*
Send in the Clowns
from *A Little Night Music*

Notable Musical Openings of the Year:

IRENE (Revival)
music by Harry Tierney and various composers, lyrics by Joseph McCarthy and various writers, book by Joseph Stein, Hugh Wheeler & Harry Rigby
opened on Broadway 3/13/73 for a run of 604 performances
selected songs: (from the 1919 Original production) Alice Blue Gown; I'm Always Chasing Rainbows; Irene; The Last Part of Ev'ry Party; Mother, Angel, Darling; The Go Wild, Simply Wild Over Me; You Made Me Love You
cast: Debbie Reynolds, Patsy Kelly, George S. Irving, Monte Markhan, Ruth Warrick, Janie Sell, Carmen Alvarez

RAISIN
music by Judd Woldin, lyrics by Robert Brittan, book by Robert Nemiroff & Charlotte Zaltzberg (Joseph Stein uncredited)
opened on Broadway 10/18/73 for a run of 847 performances
selected songs: He Come Down This Morning; Measure the Valleys; Not Anymore; Sidewalk Tree; Sweet Time; A Whole Lotta Sunlight; Whose Angry Little Man; You Done Right
cast: Virginia Capers, Joe Morton, Ernestine Jackson, Ralph Cartet, Debbie Allen, Robert Jackson, Ted Ross

A LITTLE NIGHT MUSIC
music & lyrics by Stephen Sondheim, book by Hugh Wheeler
opened on Broadway 2/25/73 for a run of 600 performances
selected songs: Every Day a Little Death; The Glamorous Life; In Praise of Women; It Would Have Been Wonderful; Liaisons; The Miller's Son; Night Waltz; Remember?; Send in the Clowns; A Weekend in the Country; You Must Meet My Wife
cast: Glynis Johns, Len Cariou, Hermione Gingold, Victoria Mallory, Laurence Guittard, Patrician Elliott, Mark Lambert, D. Jamin-Bartlett, George Lee Andrews

A Little Night Music (Martha Swope)

1974   *Featured Song Selection:*
I Won't Send Roses
From *Mack and Mabel*

Notable Musical Openings of the Year:

CANDIDE (Revival)
music by Leonard Bernstein, lyrics by Richard Wilbur and various writers, book by Hugh Wheeler
opened on Broadway 3/10/74 for a run of 740 performances
selected songs: (a revision of the original 1956 production) Auto Da Fé (What a Day); The Best of All Possible Worlds; Bon Voyage; Glitter and Be Gay; I Am Easily Assimilated; It Must Be So; Life is Happiness Indeed; Make Our Garden Grow; Oh, Happy We; This World
cast: Lewis J. Stadlin, Mark Baker, Maureen Brennan, Sam Freed, June Gable, Deborah St. Darr

THE MAGIC SHOW
music & lyrics by Stephen Schwartz, book by Bob Randall
opened on Broadway 5/28/74 for a run of 1,920 performances
selected songs: The Goldfarb Variations; Lion Tamer; Style; Up to His Old Tricks; West End Avenue
cast: Doug Henning; Dale Soules, David Ogden Stiers, Anita Morris

MACK AND MABEL
music by Jerry Herman, lyrics & book by Michael Stewart
opened on Broadway 10/6/74 for a run of 65 performances
selected songs: Big Time; Hundreds of Girls; I Promise You a Happy Ending; I Wanna Make the World Laugh; I Won't Send Roses; Movies Were Movies; Tap Your Troubles Away; Time Heals Everything; When Mabel Comes in the Room;
cast: Robert Preston, Bernadette Peters, Lisa Kirk, Jerry Dodge, Jerry Mitchell

1975   *Featured Song Selection:*
What I Did for Love
from *A Chorus Line*

Notable Musical Openings of the Year:

THE WIZ
music & lyrics by Charlie Smalls, book by William F. Brown
opened on Broadway 1/5/75 for a run of 1,672 performances
selected songs: Be a Lion; Don't Nobody Bring Me No Bad News; Ease on Down the Road; He's the Wizard; If You Believe; Slide Some Oil to Me
cast: Tiger Haynes, Ted Ross, Hinton Battle, Stephanie Mills, Clarice Taylor, Mabel King, Andre de Shields, Tasha Thomas, DeeDee Bridgewater

SHENANDOAH
music by Gary Geld, lyrics by Peter Udell, book by James Lee Barrett, with Philip Rose & Peter Udell
opened on Broadway 1/7/75 for a run of 1,050 performances
selected songs: Freedom; I've Heard It All Before; Meditation; Next to Lovin' I Like Fightin'; The Only Home I Know; The Pickers Are Comin'; Violets and Silverbells; We Make a Beautiful Pair
cast: John Cullum, Gordon Theodore, Penelope Milford, Joel Higgins, Ted Agress, Gordon Halliday, Chip Ford

A CHORUS LINE
music by Marvin Hamlisch, lyrics by Edward Kleban, conception by Michael Bennett
opened on Broadway 4/15/75 for a run of 6,137 performances
selected songs: At the Ballet; I Hope I Get It; The Music and the Mirror; Nothing; One; What I Did for Love; Dance: Ten-Looks: Three; Sing
cast: Kelly Bishop, Pamela Blair, Wayne Cilento, Kay Cole, Patricia Garland, Baayork Lee, Priscilla Lopez, Robert LuPone, Donna McKechnie, Michael Stuart, Thommie Walsh, Sammy Williams

CHICAGO
music by John Kander, lyrics by Fred Ebb, book by Fred Ebb & Bob Fosse
opened on Broadway 6/3/75 for a run of 898 performances
selected songs: All I Care About; All That Jazz; Class; Mr. Cellophane; My Own Best Friend; Nowadays; Razzle Dazzle; Roxie
cast: Gwen Verdon, Chita Rivera, Jerry Orbach, Barney Martin, Mary McCarty, M. O'Haughey, Graciela Daniele

1976   *Featured Song Selection:*
Pretty Lady
from *Pacific Overtures*

Notable Musical Openings of the Year:

PACIFIC OVERTURES
music & lyrics by Stephen Sondheim, book by John Weidman
opened on Broadway 1/11/76 for a run of 193 performances
selected songs: A Bowler Hat; Chrysanthemum Tea; Four Black Dragons; Next; Please Hello; Pretty Lady; Someone in a Tree; There Is No Other Way; Welcome to Kananawa
cast: Mako, Soon-Teck Oh, Yuki Shimoda, Sab Shimono, Isao Sato

1977   *Featured Song Selection:*
It's the Hard-Knock Life
from *Annie*

Notable Musical Openings of the Year:

ANNIE
music by Charles Strouse, lyrics by Martin Charnin, book by Thomas Meehan
opened on Broadway 4/21/77 for a run of 2,377 performances
selected songs: Annie; Easy Street; I Don't Need Anything but You; I Think I'm Gonna Like It Here; It's the Hard-Knock Life; Little Girls; Maybe; N. Y. C.; A New Deal for Christmas; Something Was Missing; Tomorrow; You're Never Fully Dressed Without a Smile
cast: Andrea McArdle, Reid Shelton, Dorothy Loudon, Sandy Faison, Robert Fitch, Barbara Erwin, Raymond Thorne, Laurie Beechman, Danielle Brisbois, Shelley Bruce

Annie (Martha Swope)

I LOVE MY WIFE
music by Cy Coleman, lyrics & book by Michael Stewart
opened on Broadway 4/17/77 for a run of 872 performances
selected songs: Everybody Is Turning On; Hey There, Good Times; I Love
My Wife; Love Revolution; Lovers on Christmas Eve; Sexually Free;
Someone Wonderful I Missed
cast: Ilene Graf, Lenny Baker, Joanna Gleason, James Naughton

THE KING AND I (Revival)
music by Richard Rodgers, lyrics & book by Oscar Hammerstein II
opened on Broadway 5/2/77 for a run of 696 performances
song same as original production (1951)
cast: Yul Brenner, Constance Towers, Michael Kermoyan, Hye-Yound Choi,
Martin Vidnovic, June Angela, Susan Kikuchi, John Michael King,
Gene Profanto, Marianne Tatum

1978 *Featured Song Selection:*
The Joint Is Jumpin'
from *Ain't Misbehavin'*

Notable Musical Openings of the Year:

ON THE TWENTIETH CENTURY
music by Cy Coleman, lyrics & book by Betty Comden & Adolph Green
opened on Broadway 2/19/78 for a run of 449 performances
selected songs: I Rise Again; Never; On the Twentieth Century; Our Private
World; Repent; Veronique; We've Got It All
cast: John Cullum, Madeline Kahn, Imogene Coca, George Coe, Dean Dittman,
Kevin Kline, Judy Kaye, George Lee Andrews

DANCIN'
music & lyrics by various writers
opened on Broadway 3/27/78 for a run of 1,774 performances
songs: 23 musical selections from Bach to Jerry Jeff Walker
cast: Sandahl Bergman, Rene Ceballos, Christopher Chadman, Wayne Cliento,
Vicki Frederick, Edward Love, Ann Reinking, Charles Ward

THE BEST LITTLE WHOREHOUSE IN TEXAS
music & lyrics by Carol Hall, book by Larry L. King & Peter Masterson
opened on Broadway 4/17/78 for a run of 1,703 performances
selected songs: Bus from Amarillo; Girl, You're a Woman; Good Old Girl;
Hard Candy Christmas; A Li'l Ole Bitty Pissant Country Place; Texas Has a
Whorehouse in It; Twenty-Four Hours of Lovin'
cast: Carlin Glynn, Henderson Forsythe, Selores Hall, Pamela Blair, Jay Garner,
Clint Allmon

AIN'T MISBEHAVIN'
music by Fats Waller, lyrics by various writers, conception by Murray Horowitz
& Richard Maltby Jr.
opened on Broadway 5/9/78 for a run of 1,604 performances
songs: 30 written or recorded by Fats Waller
cast: Nell Carter, Andre de Shields, Armelia McQueen, Ken Page,
Charlaine Woodard

Ain't Misbehavin' (Martha Swope)

I'M GETTING MY ACT TOGETHER
AND TAKING IT ON THE ROAD
music by Nancy Ford, lyrics & book by Gretchen Cryer
opened Off-Broadway 6/14/78 for a run of 1,165 performances
selected songs: Dear Tom; Happy Birthday; Miss America; Natural High;
Old Friend; Strong Woman Number
cast: Gretchen Cryer, Joel Fabiani, Betty Aberlin, Don Scardino

1979 *Featured Song Selection:*
Don't Cry for Me Argentina
from *Evita*

Notable Musical Openings of the Year:

THEY'RE PLAYING OUR SONG
music by Marvin Hamlisch, lyrics by Carol Bayer Sager, book by Neil Simon
opened on Broadway 2/11/79 for a run of 1,082 performances
selected songs: Fallin'; If He Really Knew Me; Just for Tonight; Right;
They're Playing Our Song; When You're in My Arms
cast: Lucie Arnaz, Robert Klein

SWEENEY TODD
music & lyrics by Stephen Sondheim, book by Hugh Wheeler
opened on Broadway 3/1/79 for a run of 557 performances
selected songs: The Ballad of Sweeney Todd; By the Sea; Epiphany;
Johanna; A Little Priest; Not While I'm Around; Pretty Women; The Worst
Pies in London
cast: Angela Lansbury, Len Cariou, Victor Garber, Ken Jennings,
Merle Lousie, Edmund Lyndeck, Sarah Rice

PETER PAN (Revival)
music by Mark Charlap; Jule Styne, lyrics by Carolyn Leigh; Betty Comden
& Adolph Green, play by James M. Barrie
opened on Broadway 9/6/79 for a run of 551 performances
songs: same as original production (1954)
cast: Sandy Duncan, George Rose, Beth Fowler, Arnold Soboloff,
Marsha Kramer

EVITA
music by Andrew Lloyd Webber, lyrics by Tim Rice
opened on Broadway 9/25/79 for a run of 1,567 performances
selected songs: The Actress Hasn't Learned; And the Money Kept Rolling
In; Another Suitcase in Another Hall; Buenos Aires; Dice Are Rolling; Don't
Cry for Me Argentina; High Flying Record; I'd Be Surprisingly Good for
You; A New Argentina; On This Night of a Thousand Stars; Rainbow Tour
cast: Patti LuPone, Mandy Patinkin, Bob Gunton, Mark Syers, Jane Ohringer

SUGAR BABIES
music by Jimmie McHugh and various composers, lyrics by Dorothy Fields
and various writers, conception by Ralph G. Allen & Harry Rigby
opened on Broadway 10/8/79 for a run of 1,208 performances
selected songs: A Good Old Burlesque Show; Don't Blame Me; Exactly
Like You; I Can't Give You Anything But Love; I Feel a Song Comin' On;
I'm Keeping Myself Available for You; I'm Shooting High; Mr. Banjo Man;
On the Sunny Side of the Street; Warm and Willing; You Can't Blame Your
Uncle Sammy
   cast: Mickey Rooney, Ann Miller, Sid Stone, Jack Fletcher, Ann Gillian,
   Bob Williams, Scot Stewart

OKLAHOMA! (Revival)
music by Richard Rodgers, lyrics & book by Oscar Hammerstein II
opened on Broadway 12/13/79 for a run of 293 performances
songs: same as original production (1943)
cast: Laurence Guittard, Christine Andreas, Mary Wickes, Christine
Ebersole, Martin Vidnovic, Harry Groener, Bruce Adler

1980
Featured Song Selection:
Lullaby of Broadway
from *42nd Street*

Notable Musical Openings of the Year:

BARNUM

music by Cy Coleman, lyrics by Michael Stewart, book by Mark Bramble
opened on Broadway 4/30/80 for a run of 854 performances
selected songs: Bigger Isn't Better; Black and White; The Colors of My
Life; Come Follow the Band; Join the Circus; One Brick at a Time; The
Prince of Humbug; There Is a Sucker Born Ev'ry Minute
cast: Jim Dale, Glenn Close, Marianne Tatum, Terri White, Leonard
John Crofoot, William C. Witter

42ND STREET
music by Harry Warren, lyrics by Al Dubin, book by Michael Stewart &
Mark Bramble
opened on Broadway 8/25/80 for a run of 3,486 performances
selected songs: About a Quarter to Nine; Dames; Forty-Second Street; Go
Into Your Dance; Lullaby of Broadway; Shadow Waltz; Shuffle Off to
Buffalo; We're in the Money; Young and Healthy; You're Getting to Be a
Habit With Me
cast: Jerry Orbach, Tammy Grimes, Wanda Richert, Lee Roy Reams,
Joseph Bova, Carole Cook

42nd Street (Martha Swope)

1981   *Featured Song Selection:*
And I Am Telling You I'm Not Going
from *Dreamgirls*

Notable Musical Openings of the Year:

THE PIRATES OF PENZANCE (Revival)
music by Arthur Sullivan, lyrics & book by William S. Gilbert
opened on Broadway 1/8/81 for a run of 772 performances
selected songs: (the operetta was premiered in 1879) I Am the Very Model
of a Modern Major-General; Oh, Better Far to Live and Die; Oh, Is There
Not One Maiden Breast?; Poor Wandering One; When a Felon's Not
Engaged in His Employment; When the Foeman Bares His Steel; With Cat-
Like Tread
cast: Kevin Kline, Estelle Parsons, Linda Ronstadt, George Rose, Rex Smith,
Tony Azito

SOPHISTICATED LADIES
music by Duke Ellington, lyrics by various writers, conception by
Donald McKayle
opened on Broadway 3/1/81 for a run of 767 performances
songs: 36 from the Duke Ellington catalogue
cast: Gregory Hines, Judith Jameson, Phyllis Hyman, P. J. Benjamin,
Hinton Battle, Terri Klausner, Gregg Burge, Mercedes Ellington,
Priscilla Baskerville

WOMAN OF THE YEAR
music by John Kander, lyrics by Fred Ebb, book by Peter Stone
opened on Broadway 3/29/81 for a run of 770 performances
selected songs: The Grass is Always Greener; One of the Boys; We're
Gonna Work It Out; Woman of the Year
cast: Lauren Bacall, Harry Guardino, Roderick Cook, Marilyn Cooper,
Eivind Harum, Grace Keagy, Rex Everhart, Jamie Ross

JOSEPH AND THE AMAZING TECHNICOLOR DREAMCOAT
music by Andrew Lloyd Webber, lyrics by Tim Rice
opened 11/18/81 for a run of 824 performances
selected songs: Any Dream Will Do; Benjamin Calypso; Go, Go, Go Joseph;
Joseph's Coat; One More Angel in Heaven; Pharaoh's Story; Those Canaan
Days
cast: Bill Hutton, Laurie Beechman, David, Tom Carder

DREAMGIRLS
music by Henry Krieger, lyrics & book by Tom Eyen
opened on Broadway 12/20/81 for a run of 1,522 performances
selected songs: And I Am Telling You I'm Not Going; Cadillac Car;
Dreamgirls; Fake Your Way to the Top; Hard to Say Goodbye, My Love; I
Am Changing; Steppin' to the Bad Side; When I First Saw You
cast: Obba Babatunde, Cleavant Derricks, Loretta Devine, Ben Harney,
Jennifer Holliday, Sherly Lee Ralph, Deborak Burrell

1982   *Featured Song Selection:*
Memory
from *Cats*

Notable Musical Openings of the Year:

NINE
music & lyrics by Maury Yeston, book by Arthur Kopit & Mario Fratti
opened on Broadway 5/9/82 for a run of 732 performances
selected songs: A Call from the Vatican; Be Italian; Be on Your Own;
Folies Bergères; Getting Tall; The Grand Canal; Guido's Song; My Husband
Makes Movies; Nine; Not Since Chaplin; Only With You; Simple; Unusual
Way
cast: Raul Julia, Karen Akers, Shelly Burch, Taina Elg, Lilianne Montevecchi,
Anita Morris, Kathi Moss

LITTLE SHOP OF HORRORS
music by Alan Menken, lyrics & book by Howard Ashman
opened Off-Broadway 7/27/82 for a run of 2,209 performances
selected songs: Grow for Me, Little Shop of Horrors; Skid Row;
Somewhere That's Green; Suddenly Seymour
cast: Ellen Greene, Lee Wilkof, Hy Anzell, Franc Luz, Leilani Jones

CATS
music by Andrew Lloyd Webber, lyrics based on T.S. Elliot
opened on Broadway 10/7/82 (still running 12/1/93)
selected songs: Grizabella; The Jellicle Ball; Jellicle Songs for Jellicle Cats;
Macavity; Memory; Mr. Mistoffelees; Old Deuteronomy; The Old Grumbie
Cat; The Rum Tum Tugger
cast: Betty Buckley, Rene Clemente, Harry Groener, Stephen Hanan,
Reed Jones, Christine Langer, Terrence V. Mann, Anna McNeely, Ken Page,
Timothy Scott

1983   *Featured Song Selection:*
The Best of Times
from *La Cage Aux Folles*

Notable Musical openings of the Year

ON YOUR TOES (Revival)
music by Richard Rodgers, lyrics by Lorenz Hart, book by Richard Rodgers,
Lorenz Hart & George Abbott
opened on Broadway 3/6/83 for a run of 505 performances
songs: same as original production (1936)
cast: Natalia Makarova, George S. Irving, Dina Merrill, George de la Peña,
Christine Andreas, Lara teeter, Betty Ann Grove, Peter Slutsker, Michael Vita

MY ONE AND ONLY
music by George Gershwin, lyrics by Ira Gershwin, book by Peter Stone &
Timothy S. Meyer
opened on Broadway 5/1/83 for a run of 767 performances
selected songs: Blah, Blah, Blah; Boy Wanted; Funny Face; He Loves and
She Loves; High Hat; How Long Has This Been Going On?; I Can't Be
Bothered Now; Kickin' the Clouds Away; My One and Only; Nice Work if
You Can get It; Soon; S'Wonderful; Strike Up the Band; Sweet and Low-Down
cast: Twiggy, Tommy Tune, Charles "Honi" Coles; Bruce McGill,
Denny Dillon, Roscoe Lee Brown

LA CAGE AUX FOLLES
music & lyrics by Jerry Herman, book by Harvey Fierstein
opened on Broadway 8/21/83 for a run of 1,176 performances
selected songs: The Best of Times; I Am What I Am; La Cage Aux Folles;
A Little More Mascara; Masculinity; Song on the Sand; With You on My Arm
cast: George Hearn, Gene Barry, Jay Garner, John Weiner, Elizabeth Parrish,
Leslie Stevens, William Thomas Jr., Merle Louise

ZORBA (Revival)
music by John Kander, lyrics by Fred Ebb, book by Joseph Stein
opened on Broadway 10/16/83 for a run of 362 performances
songs: same as original production, plus; Mine Song; Woman (1968)
cast: Anthony Quinn, Lila Kedrova, Robert Westenberg, Debbie Shapiro

THE TAP DANCE KID
music by Henry Krieger, lyrics by Robert Lorick, book by Charles Blackwell
opened on Broadway 12/21/83 for a run of 669 performances
selected songs: Dancing Is Everything; Fabulous Feet; Class Act; I
Remember How It Was; Dance If It Makes You Happy
cast: Hinton Battle, Samuel Wright, Hattie Winston, Alfonso Ribeiro,
Alan Weeks, Marinte Allard, Jackie Lowe

1984   *Featured Song Selections:*
Sunday
from *Sunday in the Park With George*

Notable Musical Openings of the Year:

SUNDAY IN THE PARK WITH GEORGE
music & lyrics by Stephen Sondheim, book by James Lapine
opened on Broadway 5/2/84 for a run of 604 performances
selected songs: Beautiful; Children and Art; Finishing the Hat; Move On;
Sunday; Sunday in the Park With George; We Do Not Belong Together
cast: Mandy Patinkin, Bernadette Peters, Charles Kimbrough, Barbara Bryne,
Dana Ivey, William Parry, Robert Westenberg

Sunday in the Park With George (Martha Swope)

1985   *Featured Song Selection:*
Unexpected Song
from *Song and Dance*

Notable Musical Openings of the Year:

BIG RIVER
music & lyrics by Roger Miller, book by William Hauptman
opened on Broadway 4/25/85 for a run of 1,005 performances
selected songs: Guv'ment; Leaving's Not the Only Way to Go; Muddy
Water; River in the Rain; Waiting for the Light; Worlds Apart; You Ought to
Be Here With Me
cast: Rene Auberjonois, Reathal Bean, Susan Browning,
Patti Cohenour, Gordon Connell, Bob Gunton,
Daniel H. Jenkins, Ron Richardson

SONG AND DANCE
music by Andrew Lloyd Webber, lyrics by Don Black &
Richard Maltby Jr., adaptation by Richard Maltby Jr.
opened on Broadway 9/18/85 for a run of 474 performances
selected songs: Capped Teeth and Ceasar Salad; Come
Back With the Same Look in Your Eyes; So Much to Do
in New York; Tell Me on a Sunday; Unexpected Song
cast: Bernadette Peters, Christopher d'Amboise,
Gregg Burge, Charlotte d'Amboise, Cynthia Onrubia,
Scott Wise

THE MYSTERY OF EDWIN DROOD
music, lyrics & book by Rupert Holmes
opened on Broadway 12/2/85 for a run of 608 performances
selected songs: Both Sides of the Coin; Ceylon; Don't
Quit While You're Ahead; Moonfall; No Good Can Come
From Bad; Off the the Races; Perfect Strangers;
The Wages of Sin
cast: George Rose, Cleo Laine, Betty Buckley,
Howard McGillin,
Patti Cohenour, Jana Schneider, John Herrera,
Jerome Dempsey

1986   *Featured Song Selection:*
Leaning on a Lamp-post
from *Me and My Gal*

Notable Musical Openings of the Year:

SWEET CHARITY (Revival)
music by Cy Coleman, lyrics by Dorothy Fields, book by
Neil Simon
opened on Broadway 4/27/86 for a run of 368 performances
songs: same as original production (1966)
cast: Debbie Allen, Michael Rupert, Bebe Neuwirth,
Allison Williams, Lee Wilkof, Mark Jacoby,
Irving Allen Lee

ME AND MY GIRL
music by Noel Gay, lyrics by Douglas Furber & various
writers, book by L. Arthur Rose & Douglas Furber,
revised by Stephen Fry
opened on Broadway 8/10/86 for a run of 1,412 performances
selected songs: The Family Solicitor; Hold My Hand; The
Lambeth Walk; Leaning on a Lamp-post; Love Makes the
World Go Round; Me and My Girl; Once You Lose Your Heart; The Sun
Has Got His Hat On; Take It on the Chin; Thinking of No-One But Me
cast: Robert Lindsay, Maryann Plunkett, George S. Irving, Jane Connell,
Jane Summerhays, Nick Ullett, Timothy Jerome, Thomas Toner,
Justine Jonston, Elizabeth Larner

1987   *Featured Song Selection:*
Bring Him Home
from *Les Misérables*

Notable Musical Openings of the Year:

STARLIGHT EXPRESS
music by Andrew Lloyd Webber, lyrics by Richard Stilgoe
opened on Broadway 3/15/87 for a run of 761 performances
selected songs: Engine of Love; I Am the Starlight; Light at the End of the
Tunnel; Make Up My Heart; One Rock and Roll Too Many; Only You;
Pumping Iron; Rolling Stone; Starlight Express
cast: Ken Ard, Jamie Beth Chandler, Steve Fowler, Jane Krakowski,
Andrea McArdle, Greg Mowry, Reva Rive, Robert Torti

ANYTHING GOES (Revival)
music & lyrics by Cole Porter, book by Timothy Crouse & John Weidman
based on original by P. G. Wodehouse & Guy Bolton, Howard Lindsay &
Russel Crouse
opened on Broadway 10/13/87 for a run of 804 performances
songs: same as original 1934 production plus Easy to Love; Friendship;
Goodbye, Little Dream, Goodbye; I Want to Row on the Crew; It's De-
Lovely; No Cure Like Travel
cast: Patti LuPone, Howard McGillan, Bill McCutcheon, Rex Everhart,
Anne Francine, Linda Hart, Anthony Heald, Kathleen Mahony-Bennett

LES MISÉRABLES
Music by Claude-Michel Schönberg, lyrics by Herbert Kretzmer, conception
by Alain Boublil & Claude Michel Schönberg
opened on Broadway 3/12/87 (still running 12/1/93)
selected songs: Bring Him Home; Castle on a Cloud; Drink With Me; Do
You Hear the People Sing?; Empty Chairs at Empty Tables; I Dreamed a
Dream; In My Life; A Little Fall of Rain; Master of the House; On My Own;
Red and Black; Who Am I?
cast: Colm Wilkinson, Terrence Mann, Randy Graff, Michael Maguire,
Leo Burmeister, Frances Ruffelle, David Bryant, Judy Kuhn, Jennifer Butt,
Braden Danner

Les Misérables (Trench/Marshak)

33

INTO THE WOODS

music & lyrics by Stephen Sondheim, book by James Lapine
opened on Broadway 11/5/87 for a run of 764 performances
selected songs: Agony; Any Moment; Children Will Listen; Giants in the
Sky; Hello, Little Girl; I Know Things Now; Into the Woods; It Takes Two;
Last Midnight; No More; No One Is Alone; Stay With Me
cast: Bernadette Peters, Joanna Gleason, Chip Zien, Tom Aldredge,
Robert Westenberg, Barbara Byrne, Kim Crosby, Danielle Ferland,
Merle Louise, Ben Wright, Joy Franz, Edmund Lyndeck, Lay McClelland,
Lauren Mitchell

1988   *Featured Song Selection:*
The Music of the Night
from *The Phantom of the Opera*

Notable Musical Openings of the Year:

CHESS

music by Benny Anderson & Bjorn Ulvaeus, lyrics by Tim Rice, book by
Richard Nelson, based on an idea by Tim Rice
opened on Broadway 4/28/88 for a run of 68 performances
selected songs: Anthem; Endgame; Heaven Help My Heart; I Know Him So
Well; Nobody's Side; One Night in Bangkok; Pity the Child; Quartet;
Someone Else's Story; The Story of Chess; Terrace Duet; You and I
cast: Judy Kuhn, David Carroll, Philip Casnoff, Dennis Parlato,
Marcia Mitzman, Paul Harman, Harry Goz, Ann Crumb

THE PHANTOM OF THE OPERA

music by Andrew Lloyd Webber, lyrics by Charles Hart & Richard Stilgoe,
book by Richard Stilgoe & Andrew Lloyd Webber
opened on Broadway 1/26/88 (still running 12/1/93)
selected songs: All I Ask of You; Angel of Music; Masquerade; The Music
of the Night; The Point of No Return; Prima Donna; Think of Me; Wishing You Were Somehow Here Again
cast: Michael Crawford, Sarah Brightman, Steve Barton, Judy Kaye,
Cris Groenendaal, Nicholas Wyman, Leila Martin, David Romano,
Elisa Heinsohn, George Lee Andrews

The Phantom of the Opera (Clive Barda)

1989   *Featured Song Selection:*
Bonjour Amour
from *Grand Hotel*

Notable Musical Openings of the Year:

JEROME ROBBINS' BROADWAY

music & lyrics by various writers
opened on Broadway 2/26/89 for a run of 633 performances
selected songs: Charleston; Comedy Tonight; Fiddler on the Roof (scenes);
I'm Flying; Mr Monotony; New York, New York; On Sunday by the Sea
(ballet); The Small House of Uncle Thomas; West Side Story (dances); You
Gotta Have a Gimmick;
cast: Jason Alexander, Charlotte d'Amboise, Susann Fletcher,
Susan Kikuchi, Michael Kubala, Robert LaFosse, Jane Lanier, Joey McKneely,
Luis Perez, Faith Prince, Debbie Shapiro, Scott Wise

GRAND HOTEL

music & lyrics by Robert Wright, George Forest & Maury Yeston, book by
Luther Davis, based on Vicki Baum's *Grand Hotel*
opened on Broadway 11/12/89 for a run of 1,018 performances
selected songs: As It Should Be; At the Grand Hotel; Bonjour Amour; The
Boston Merger; The Grand Parade; I Waltz Alone; I Want to Go to
Hollywood; Love Can't Happen; Roses at the Station; Some Have, Some
Have Not; Villa on a Hill; Who Couldn't Dance With You
cast: John Wylie, Yvonne Marceau, Pierre Dulaine, Timothy Jerome,
Jane Krakowski, Michael Jeter

GYPSY (Revival)

music by Jule Styne, lyrics by Stephen Sondheim, book by Arthur Laurents
opened on Broadway 11/16/89 for a run of 477 performances
songs: same as original production (1959)
cast: Tyne Daly, Crista Moore, Tracy Venner, Robert Lambert,
Jonathan Hadary, John Remme

CITY OF ANGELS

music by Cy Coleman, lyrics by David Zippel, book by Larry Gelbart
opened on Broadway 12/11/89 for a run of 878 performances
selected songs: All Ya Have To Do Is Wait; The Buddy System; Double
Talk; Everybody's Gotta be Somewhere; It Needs Work; What You Don't
Know About Women; With Each Breath I Take; You Can Count On Me;
You're Nothing Without Me
cast: James Naughton, Gregg Edelmann, Randy Graff, Dee Hoty,
Kay McClelland, Rene Auberjonois

1990   *Featured Song Selection:*
Love Changes Everything
from *Aspects of Love*

Notable Musical Openings of the Year:

ASPECTS OF LOVE

music by Andrew Lloyd Weber, lyrics by Don Black & Charles Hart, book
by Andrew Lloyd Weber, based on the novel by David Garnett
opened on Broadway 4/8/90 for a run of 377 performances
selected songs: Anything But Lonely; The First Man You Remember; Love
Changes Everything; A Memory of Happy Moments; Other Pleasures;
Seeing is Believing; She'd Be Far Better Off With You
cast: Ann Crumb, Michael Ball, Kevin Colson, Walter Charles,
Kathleen Rowe McAllen, Deanna DuClos, Dannielle Du Clos

ONCE ON THIS ISLAND

music by Stephen Flaherty, lyrics & book by Lynn Ahrend (Based on "My
Love, My Love" by Rosa Guy)
opened on Broadway 10/18/90 for a run of 469 performances
selected songs: And the Gods Heard Her Prayer; Forever Yours; Mama Will
Provide; One Small Girl; Pray; The Sad Tale of Beauzhommes; Some Girls;
We Dance; Why We Tell the Story
cast: Jerry Dixon, Andrea Frierson, Sheila Gibbs, La Chanze,
Kecia Lewis-Evans, Afi McMlendon, Gerry McIntyre, Milton Craig Nealy,
Nikki Rene, Eric Reiley, Ellis E. Williams

ASSASSINS

music & lyrics by Stephen Sondheim, book by John Weidman
opened on Broadway 12/18/90 for a run of 73 performances
selected songs: Another National Anthem; The Ballad of Booth; The Ballad
of Czolgosz; The Ballad of Guiteau; Everybody's Got the Right; Gun Song;
How I Saved Roosevelt; November 22, 1963; Unworthy of Your Love;
You Can Close the New York Stock Exchange
cast: Jane Alexander, Patrick Cassidy, Annie Golden, Victor Garber,
Terrence Mann, Greg Germann, Jonathon Hadary, Eddie Korbich,
Lee Wilkof, Debra Monk

1991   *Featured Song Selection:*
Sun and Moon
from *Miss Saigon*

Notable Musical Openings of the Year:

THE SECRET GARDEN

music by Lucy Simon, lyrics & book by Marsha Norman, based on the novel
by Frances Hodgson Burnett
opened on Broadway 4/25/91 for a run of 706 performances
selected songs: Come Spirit, Come Charm; A Fine White Horse; The Girl I
Mean to Be; The House Upon the Hill; How Could I Ever Know?; I Heard
Someone Crying; Lily's Eyes; Round Shouldered Man; Show Me the Key;
There's a Girl
cast: John Babcock, Daisy Eagan, Allison Fraser, Rebecca Luker,
John Cameron Mitchell, Mandy Patinkin, Barbara Rosenblatt, Tom Toner,
Robert Westenberg

MISS SAIGON

music by Claude-Michel Schönberg, lyrics by Richard Maltby Jr. &
Alain Boublil; adapted from original French lyrics by Alain Boublil;
additional material by Richard Maltby Jr.
opened on Broadway 4/11/91 (still running 12/1/93)
selected songs: The American Dream; The Heat Is On In Saigon; I'd Give
My Life for You; The Last Night of the World; The Morning of the Dragon;
The Movie In My Mind; Sun and Moon; What a Waste Why God Why
cast: Jonathon Pryce, Lea Salonga, Hinton Battle, Willy Falk, Barry K. Bernal,
Liz Calloway, Kam Cheng

Miss Saigon (Trench/Marcus)

Guys and Dolls (Boneau/Bryan-Brown)

THE WILL ROGERS FOLLIES
music by Cy Coleman, lyrics by Betty Comden & Adolph Green, book by Peter Stone
opened on Broadway 5/1/91 for a run of 983 performances
selected songs: Give a Man Enough Rope; Just a Coupla Indian Boys; My Unknown Someone; Never Met a Man I Didn't Like; No Man Left For Me; Once In a While; Will-a-Mania; Without You
cast: Keith Carradine, Dee Hoty, Dick Letessa, Cady Huffman, Vince Bruce, Paul Ukena Jr., and the voice of Gregory Peck

1992   *Featured Song Selection:*
Embraceable You
from *Crazy for You*

Notable Musical Openings of the Year:

CRAZY FOR YOU
music by George Gershwin, lyrics by Ira Gershwin, book by Ken Ludwig; co-conceived by Ken Ludwig and Mike Ockrent; inspired by material by Guy Bolton and John McGowan
opened on Broadway 2/19/92 (still running 12/1/93)
selected songs: Bidin' My Time; But Not For Me; Could You Use Me; Embraceable You; I Can't Be Bothered Now; I Got Rhythm; K-ra-zy for You; Naughty Baby; Nice Work if You Can Get It; The Real American Folk Song (Is a Rag); Shall We Dance?; Slap That Bass; Someone to Watch Over Me; Stiff Upper Lip; They Can't Take That Away from Me; Things Are Looking Up; Tonight's the Night; What Causes That?;
cast: Harry Groener, Jodi Benson, Beth Leavel, Bruce Adler, Jane Connell, John Hillner, Irene Pawk, Stephen Temperly, Amelia White, The Manhattan Rhythm Kings

FIVE GUYS NAMED MOE
music & lyrics by various composers and writers, book by Clarke Peters
opened on Broadway 7/1/92 for a run of 445 performances
selected songs: Ain't Nobody Here But Us Chickens; Beware, Brother, Beware; Choo, Choo, Ch'boogie; Early in the Morning; I Like 'Em Fat Like That; Is You Or Is You Ain't My Baby; Push Ka Pi Shi Pie
cast: Jerry Dixon, Doug Eskew, Milton Craig Nealy, Kevin Ramsey, Jeffrey D. Sams, Glen Turner

GUYS AND DOLLS (Revival)
music & lyrics by Frank Loesser, book by Joe Swerling & Abe Burrows
opened on Broadway 4/14/92 (still running 12/1/93)
songs: same as original production
cast: Peter Gallagher, Nathan Lane, Josie de Guzman, Faith Prince, Walter Bobbie, John Carpenter, Steve Ryan, Ernie Sabella, J. K. Simmons, Herschel Sparber, Gary Chryst, Scott Wise

JELLY'S LAST JAM
music by Jelly Roll Morton, adapted by Luther Henderson; additional original music by Luther Henderson, lyrics by Susan Birkenhead, book by George C. Wolfe
opened on Broadway 4/26/92 for a run of 569 performances
selected songs: The Chicago Stomp; The Creole Way; Dr. Jazz; Good Ole New York; In My Day; Jelly's Jam; The Last Rites; Lonely Boy Blues; Lovin' Is a Lowdown Blues; Michigan Water; Play the Music for Me; Something More; That's How You Jazz; That's the Way We Do Things in New Yawk; Too Late Daddy; The Whole World's Waitin' to Sing Your Song
cast: Gregory Hines, Keith David, Savion Glover, Stanley Wayne Mathis, Toyna Pinkins, Mary Bond Davis, Ann Duquesnay, Mamie Duncan-Gibbs, Stephanie Pope, Rueben Santiago-Hudson, Allison Williams

FALSETTOS
music & lyrics by William Flynn, book by William Flynn & James Lapine
opened on Broadway 10/1/92 for a run of 486 performances
selected songs: Everyone Hates His Parents; Four Jews in a Room Bitching; I'm Breaking Down; I Never Wanted to Love You; Love is Blind; Making a Home; March of the Falsettos; Thrill of First Love; A Tight Knit Family; Unlikely Lovers; What Would I Do
cast: Michael Rupert, Stephen Bogardus, Chip Zien, Barbara Walsh, Heather Mac Rae, Carrolee Carmello, Jonathan Kaplan, Andrew Harrison Leeds

1993   *Featured Song Selection:*
The Kiss of the Spider Woman
from *The Kiss of the Spider Woman*

Notable Musical Openings of the Year:

THE GOODBYE GIRL
music by Marvin Hamlisch, lyrics by David Zippel, book by Neil Simon
opened on Broadway 3/3/93 for a run of 188 performances
selected songs: A Beat Behind; Don't Follow in My Footsteps; Good News, Bad News; How Can I Win?; I Can Play this Part; My Rules; No More; Paula; What a Guy
cast: Bernadette Peters, Martin Short

TOMMY
music & lyrics by Peter Townsend and The Who
opened on Broadway 4/22/93 (still running 12/1/93)
selected songs: Pinball Wizard; See Me, Feel Me; Fiddle About; I'm Free; Acid Queen

THE KISS OF THE SPIDER WOMAN
music by John Kander, lyrics by Fred Ebb, book by Terrence McNally
opened on Broadway 5/3/93 (still running 12/1/93)
selected songs: Anything for Him; The Day After That; Dear One, Dressing Them Up; I Do Miracles; The Kiss of the Spider Woman; The Morphine Tango; Only in the Movies; She's a Woman; Where Are You
cast: Chita Rivera, Brent Carver, Anthony Crivello

SHE LOVES ME (Revival)
music by Jerry Bock, lyrics by Sheldon Harnick, book by Joe Masteroff
opened on Broadway 6/10/93 (still running, after a brief hiatus, 10/1/93)
selected songs: same as the original production (1963)
cast: Judy Kuhn, Boyd Gaines, Brad Kane, Jonathan Freeman, Sally Mayes, Howard McGillin

After the Ball
interpolated into A TRIP TO CHINATOWN

Words amd Music by
CHARLES K. HARRIS

Arr. by JOS. CLAUDER.

Copyright © 1993 by HAL LEONARD PUBLISHING CORPORATION
International Copyright Secured   All Rights Reserved

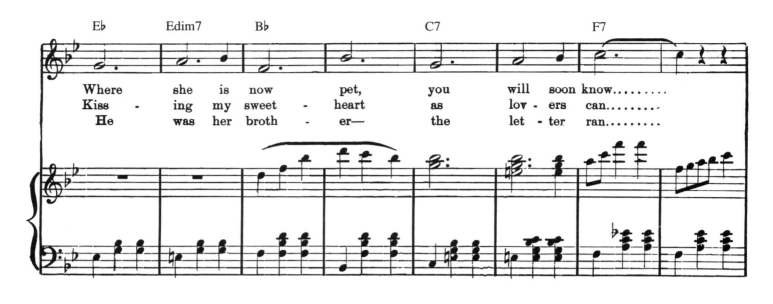

Where she is now pet, you will soon know.........
Kiss - ing my sweet - heart as lov - ers can.........
He was her broth - er— the let - ter ran.........

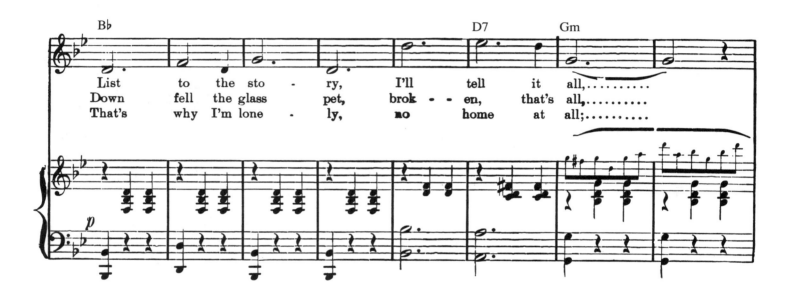

List to the sto - ry, I'll tell it all,..........
Down fell the glass pet, brok - - en, that's all,..........
That's why I'm lone - ly, no home at all;..........

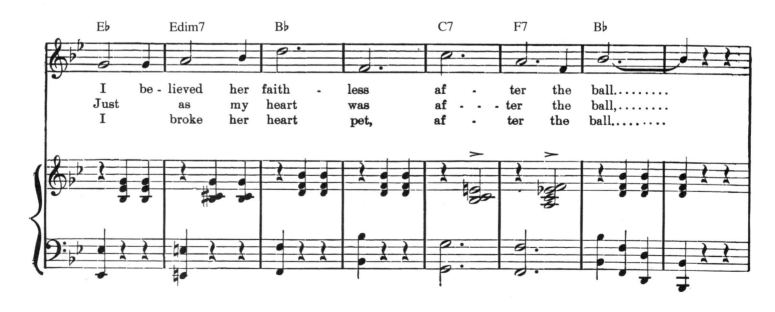

I be - lieved her faith - less af - ter the ball.........
Just as my heart was af - - - ter the ball,.........
I broke her heart pet, af - ter the ball.........

You're a Grand Old Flag
from GEORGE WASHINGTON, JR.

Words and Music by George M. Cohan

Tempo di Marcia

There's a feel-ing comes a-steal-ing, and it sets my brain a-reel-ing, When I'm
I'm a crank-y hank-y pank-y, I'm a dead square, hon-est Yan-kee, And I'm

list'-ning to the mu-sic of a mil-i-ta-ry band; An-y tune like "Yan-kee
might-y proud of that old flag that flies for Un-cle Sam; Though I don't be-lieve in

Revisions by Mary Cohan.

Copyright © 1993 by HAL LEONARD PUBLISHING CORPORATION
International Copyright Secured   All Rights Reserved

1896

42

Gypsy Love Song

from THE FORTUNE TELLER

Lyrics by HARRY B. SMITH
Music by VICTOR HERBERT

Molto tranquillo

1 The birds of the for-est are call-ing for thee,__ And the
2 The fawn that you tamed has a look in its eyes__ That doth

shades and the glades are lone-ly;__ Sum-mer is there with her blos-soms
say: "We are too long part-ed;" Songs that are trolled by our com-rades

fair,__ And you__ are ab-sent on-ly.__ No
old,__ Are not now, as they were,__ light-heart-ed.__ The

Copyright © 1993 by HAL LEONARD PUBLISHING CORPORATION
International Copyright Secured   All Rights Reserved

bird__ that nests in the green-wood tree,__ But sighs to greet you and
wild rose fades in the leaf - y shades, Its ghost will find you and

kiss you, All the vi-o-lets yearn, yearn for your safe re-turn, But
haunt you, All the friends say: "Come, come to your wood-land home," And

most of all__ I miss you.__
most of all__ I want you.__

REFRAIN

Andante

Slum - ber on, my lit-tle gyp-sy sweet-heart, Dream of the field and the

p dolcissimo

grove,_____ Can you hear me, hear me in that dream-land,

Where your fan – cies rove? Slum - ber on, my

lit - tle gyp-sy sweet-heart, Wild lit-tle wood - land dove,

Can you hear the song_ that_tells you All my_heart's true love?_____

Tell Me Pretty Maiden

from FLORODORA

By LESLIE STUART.

Copyright © 1993 by HAL LEONARD PUBLISHING CORPORATION
International Copyright Secured   All Rights Reserved

must love some one, real-ly And it might as well be you!
must love some one, real-ly And it might as well be you!

Toyland

from BABES IN TOYLAND

Lyrics by GLEN MacDONOUGH
Music by VICTOR HERBERT

Very slow and dreamily

When
you've grown up, my dears ___ And are as old as I ___ You'll
you've grown up, my dears ___ There comes a drear-y day ___ When

oft-en pon-der on the years That roll so swift-ly by, my dears, that
'mid the locks of black ap-pears The first pale gleam of gray, my dears, the

Copyright © 1993 by HAL LEONARD PUBLISHING CORPORATION
International Copyright Secured   All Rights Reserved

Give My Regards to Broadway

from LITTLE JOHNNY JONES

Music and Lyrics by
GEORGE M. COHAN

Copyright © 1993 by HAL LEONARD PUBLISHING CORPORATION
International Copyright Secured   All Rights Reserved

CHORUS.

Give my re - gards to Broad - - way, re -

mem - ber me to Her - ald Square,____

Tell all the gang at For - ty - Sec - ond street, that

I will soon be there;____

How'd You Like to Spoon With Me?

from THE EARL AND THE GIRL

Words by EDWARD LASKA
Music by JEROME KERN

Copyright © 1905 PolyGram International Publishing, Inc.
Copyright Renewed
International Copyright Secured   All Rights Reserved

Vilia

from THE MERRY WIDOW

Original German Words by
VIKTOR LEON and LEO STEIN
English Version by
MARTHA GERHART
Music by FRANZ LEHÁR

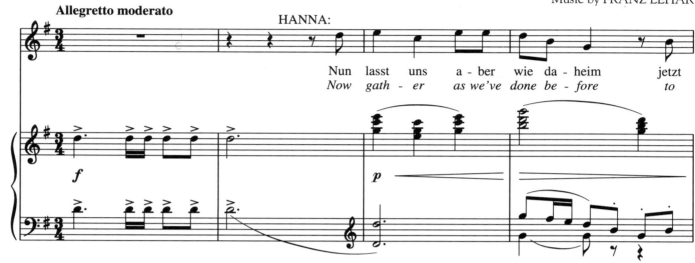

Nun lasst uns a - ber wie da - heim jetzt
Now gath - er as we've done be - fore to

sin - gen un - sern Rin - gel reim von ei - ner Fee, die wie be - kannt, da - heim die
sing our fa - v'rite song of yore a-bout a maid of wide-spread fame; you know that

Vil - ja wird ge - nannt!
Vil - lia was her name!

Copyright © 1993 by HAL LEONARD PUBLISHING CORPORATION
International Copyright Secured   All Rights Reserved

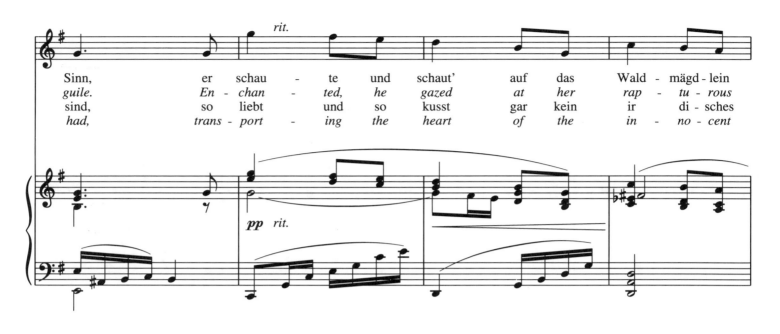

Sinn, er schau - te und schaut' auf das Wald - mägd - lein
guile. En - chan - ted, he gazed at her rap - tu - rous
sind, so liebt und so kusst gar kein ir - di - sches
had, trans - port - ing the heart of the in - no - cent

hin. Und ein nie ge - kann - ter Schau - er fasst' den jun - gen Jä - gers-
smile. Then with un - ex - pect - ed feel - ing — pas - sion he could not de-
Kind. Als sie sich dann satt ge - küsst ver schwand sie zu der sel - ben
lad. But, be - fore the lad could tell, she van - ished in the mis - ty

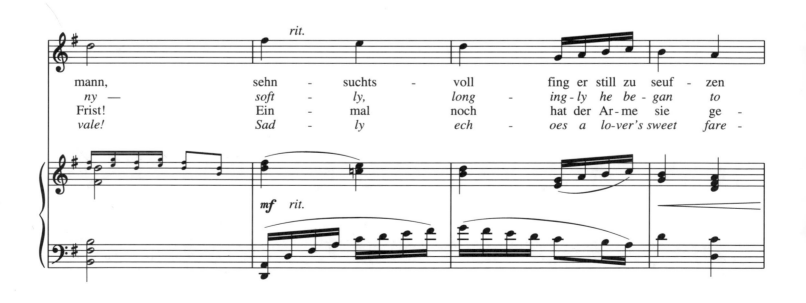

mann, sehn - suchts - voll fing er still zu seuf - zen
ny — soft - ly, long - ing - ly he be - gan to
Frist! Ein - mal noch hat der Ar - me sie ge-
vale! Sad - ly ech - oes a lo-ver's sweet fare-

an?
why,
Bang fleht ein lieb - kran - ker Mann!
in your em - bra - ces, I die!

Vil - ja, o Vil - ja, was thust Du mir
Vi - lia, oh Vi - lia, will love tell me

(opt. 2nd time)

Italian Street Song
from NAUGHTY MARIETTA

Lyric by
RIDA JOHNSON YOUNG

Music by
VICTOR HERBERT

Copyright © 1993 by HAL LEONARD PUBLISHING CORPORATION
International Copyright Secured   All Rights Reserved

sweet, the pleas - ant fall of dan - cing feet, Oh! could I re-

turn, oh! joy com-plete! Na-po-li, Na-po-li, Na-po-li!

NOTE-OBBLIGATO TO BE SUNG WITH 2nd CHORUS ONLY

Allegro moderato

Oh

Zing, zing, ziz-zy, ziz-zy, zing, zing, Boom, boom, aye. Zing, zing,

ziz-zy, ziz-zy, zing, zing, Man-do-li-nas gay. Zing, zing, ziz-zy, ziz-zy, zing, zing,

Boom, boom, aye, La, la, la, Ha, ha, ha, Zing, boom aye.

La, la; la, la, ha, ha, ha, zing, zing, aye._____ aye._____ aye._____

A to B may omited

La, la, la, la _____

La, la, la, la, _____

1911

Woodman, Woodman, Spare That Tree

Words amd Music by IRVING BERLIN
and VINCENT BRYAN

© Copyright 1911 by Irving Berlin
Copyright Renewed
International Copyright Secured   All Rights Reserved

Giannina Mia
from THE FIREFLY

Lyrics by OTTO HARBACH
Music by RUDOLF FRIML

Copyright © 1993 by HAL LEONARD PUBLISHING CORPORATION
International Copyright Secured   All Rights Reserved

They Didn't Believe Me

from THE GIRL FROM UTAH

Words by HERBERT REYNOLDS
Music by JEROME KERN

Andante moderato

1. *He:* Got the cut - est lit - tle way, ___ Like to watch you all the
2. *She:* Don't know how it hap - pened quite, ___ May have been the sum - mer

day ___ And it cer - tain - ly seems fine ___ Just to think that you'll be
night ___ May have been, well, who can say ___ Things just hap - pen an - y

mine. ___ When I see your pret - ty smile ___
way, ___ All I know is I said "yes!" ___

Copyright © 1914 PolyGram International Publishing, Inc.
Copyright Renewed
International Copyright Secured   All Rights Reserved

I Love a Piano

from STOP! LOOK! LISTEN!

Words and Music by
IRVING BERLIN

© Copyright 1915 by Irving Berlin
Copyright Renewed
International Copyright Secured   All Rights Reserved

thought was sim-ply di - vine.
who don't know when to pause.

But to-day, when they play, I could
At her best I de-test the so -

hiss them.
pran - o,

Ev - 'ry bar is a jar to my sys - tem.
but I run to the one at the pian - o.

But
I

there's one
al - ways

mu - si - cal in - stru-ment, that I
love the ac-comp - 'ni - ment and that's

call
be -

mine.
cause,

I love a pian - o,

I love a

Till the Clouds Roll By

from OH BOY!

Words by P.G. WODEHOUSE
Music by JEROME KERN

Allegretto

She: I'm so sad to think that I have had to drive you from your home so

She: What bad luck, It's com-ing down in buck-ets; Have you an um-brel-la

cool-ly. He: I'd be gain-ing noth-ing by re-main-ing,

hand-y? He: I've a warm coat, wat-er-proof, a storm coat,

Copyright © 1917 PolyGram International Publishing, Inc.
Copyright Renewed
International Copyright Secured   All Rights Reserved

Rock-a-Bye Your Baby With a Dixie Melody

from SINBAD

Lyric by SAM M. LEWIS and JOE YOUNG
Music by JEAN SCHWARTZ

© 1918 MILLS MUSIC, INC.
© Renewed 1946 MPL COMMUNICATIONS, INC. and WAROCK CORP.
All Rights Reserved

A Pretty Girl Is Like a Melody

from ZIEGFELD FOLLIES

Words and Music
IRVING BERLI

© Copyright 1919 by Irving Berlin
Copyright Renewed
International Copyright Secured   All Rights Reserved

Look For the Silver Lining

from SALLY

Words by BUDDY DeSYLVA
Music by JEROME KERN

Moderato

Boy: Please don't be of-fend-ed if I preach to you a while,
Girl: As I wash my dish-es, I'll be fol-low-ing your plan,

Tears are out of place in eyes that were meant to smile.
Till I see the bright-ness in ev-'ry pot and pan.

Copyright © 1920 PolyGram International Publishing, Inc. and Stephen Ballentine Publishing
Copyright Renewed
International Copyright Secured   All Rights Reserved

Everybody Step
from MUSIC BOX REVUE

Words and Music by
IRVING BERLIN

Soon _____ you'll hear a tune, _____ that's gon - na lift you out of your seat.

It could be sweet-er but then the me - ter was

© Copyright 1921 by Irving Berlin
Copyright Renewed
International Copyright Secured   All Rights Reserved

I'll Build a Stairway to Paradise

from GEORGE WHITE'S SCANDALS

Words by B.G. DESYLVA and IRA GERSHWIN
Music by GEORGE GERSHWIN

All you Preach-ers Who de-light in pan-ning the danc-ing teach-ers Let me tell you there are a lot of fea-tures

© 1922 WB MUSIC CORP. (Renewed)
Rights for the Extended Renewal Term in the United States controlled by WB MUSIC CORP. and STEPHEN BALLENTINE MUSIC
Rights for STEPHEN BALLENTINE MUSIC administered by THE SONGWRITERS GUILD OF AMERICA
All Rights Reserved

Indian Love Call

from ROSE-MARIE

Lyrics by OTTO HARBACH and OSCAR HAMMERSTEIN II
Music by RUDOLF FRIML

© 1924 (Renewed) WARNER BROS. INC., OTTO HARBACH PUB. DES. and OSCAR HAMMERSTEIN III PUB. DES.
All Rights Reserved

Manhattan

from GARRICK GAIETIES

Words by LORENZ HART
Music by RICHARD RODGERS

Copyright © 1925 by Edward B. Marks Music Company
Copyright Renewed
International Copyright Secured   All Rights Reserved
Used by Permission

Refrain (gaily, but not fast)

We'll have Man-hat - tan, The Bronx and Stat - en Is - land too;____
We'll go to Green-wich Where mod - ern men itch To be free;____
We'll go to Yonk- ers Where true love con-quers In the wilds;____
We'll have Man-hat - tan The Bronx and Stat - en Is - land '00;____

____ It's love-ly go-ing through____ the Zoo;_____
____ And Bowl-ing Green you'll see_____ with me;_____
____ And starve to - geth-er, dear_____ in Childs'_____
____We'll try to cross Fifth Av - - en - ue;_____

It's ver - y fan - cy On old De - lan - cey Street, you know;____
We'll bathe at Bright- on, The fish you'll fright - en When you're in;____
We'll go to Cone - y And eat bo - logn - y on a roll;____
As black as on - yx We'll find the Bron - nix Park Ex - press;____

by; _____ The great big cit - y's a won-d'rous toy Just
view; _____ The cit - y's bus - tle can-not de - stroy The
close; _____ The cit - y's clam-or can nev - er spoil The
end _____ But Civ - ic Vir - tue can-not de - stroy The

made for a girl and boy, We'll turn Man-hat-tan In - to an isle of
dreams of a girl and boy, We'll turn Man-hat-tan In - to an isle of
dreams of a boy and goil, We'll turn Man-hat-tan In - to an isle of
dreams of a girl and boy, We'll turn Man-hat-tan In - to an isle of

joy. _____
joy. _____
joy. _____

joy. _____

Someone to Watch Over Me

from OH, KAY!

Music and Lyrics by
GEORGE and IRA GERSHWIN

There's a say-ing old Says that love is blind, Still we're of-ten told "Seek and ye shall find". So I'm going to seek A cer-tain lad I've had in mind.

© 1926 WB MUSIC CORP. (Renewed)
All Rights Reserved

Ol' Man River

from SHOW BOAT

Lyrics by OSCAR HAMMERSTEIN II
Music by JEROME KERN

Col-ored folks work on de Mis-sis-sip-pi, Col-ored folks work while de white folks play,

Pull-in' dose boats from de dawn to sun-set, Git-tin' no rest till de judg-ment day.

Copyright © 1927 PolyGram International Publishing, Inc.
Copyright Renewed
International Copyright Secured   All Rights Reserved

I Can't Give You Anything But Love

from BLACKBIRDS OF 1928

Words by DOROTHY FIELDS
Music by JIMMY McHUGH

Copyright © 1928 ALDI MUSIC and IRENEADELE MUSIC
Copyright Renewed
Pursuant to Sections 304(c) and 401(b) of the U.S. Copyright Law.
International Copyright Secured   All Rights Reserved

Why Was I Born?

from SWEET ADELINE

Lyrics by OSCAR HAMMERSTEIN II
Music by JEROME KERN

Copyright © 1929 PolyGram International Publishing, Inc.
Copyright Renewed
International Copyright Secured   All Rights Reserved

Dream-ing that you're be - side me, I pic - ture the pret - ti - est sto - ries on - ly to wake up,_____ All by my - self._____

What is the good of me, by my - self?_____ *L.H.*

poco rit

Refrain

Why was I born?_____ Why am I

p a tempo

con pedale

Love For Sale

from THE NEW YORKERS

Words and Music by
COLE PORTER

© 1930 WARNER BROS. INC. (Renewed)
All Rights Reserved

Who Cares?
(So Long As You Care For Me)
from OF THEE I SING

Music and Lyrics by GEORGE GERSHWIN
and IRA GERSHWIN

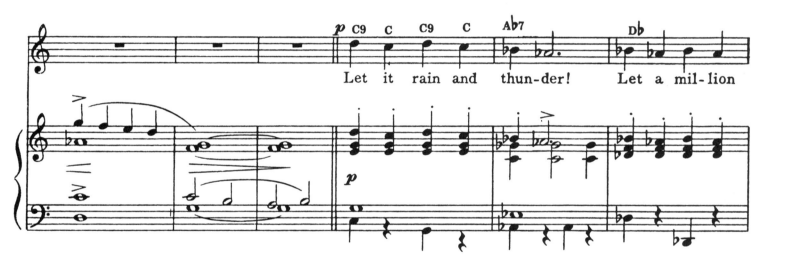

Let it rain and thun-der! Let a mil-lion

firms go un-der! _____ I am not con-cerned with

© 1931 WB MUSIC CORP. (Renewed)
All Rights Reserved

1931

146

The Song Is You

from MUSIC IN THE AIR

Lyrics by OSCAR HAMMERSTEIN II
Music by JEROME KERN

I hear mu-sic when I look at you, _____ A beau-ti-ful

theme of ev-'ry dream I ev-er knew, _____ Down deep in my

heart, _____ I hear it play, _____ I feel it

Copyright © 1932 PolyGram International Publishing, Inc.
Copyright Renewed
International Copyright Secured   All Rights Reserved

Supper Time
from AS THOUSANDS CHEER

Words and Music by
IRVING BERLIN

Sup-per time, ___ I should set the ta - ble 'cause it's sup-per time. ___

Some-how I'm not a - ble 'cause that man o' - mine ___ ain't com-in' home ___ no

© Copyright 1933 by Irving Berlin
Copyright Renewed
International Copyright Secured   All Rights Reserved

1933

more. _____ Sup-per time, _____

kids will soon be yell - in' for their sup - per time. _____ How'll I keep from tell - in' that that

man o' - mine ____ ain't com - in' home _ no more. _____

How'll I keep ex-plain-in' when they ask me where he's

155

You're the Top
from ANYTHING GOES

Words and Music by
COLE PORTER

At words po-et-ic I'm so pa-thet-ic that I al-ways have found it best, In-stead of get-ting 'em off my chest, to let 'em rest un-ex-pressed. I hate pa-rad-ing my ser-e-nad-ing As I'll prob-a-bly miss a bar, But

© 1934 WARNER BROS. INC. (Renewed)
All Rights Reserved

159

My Romance

from JUMBO

Words by LORENZ HART
Music by RICHARD RODGERS

Copyright © 1935 PolyGram International Publishing, Inc.
Copyright Renewed
The interest of Richard Rodgers for the extended term of copyright assigned to the Rodgers Family Partnership
(Administered by Williamson Music)
Rights on behalf of the Estate of Lorenz Hart administered by WB Music Corp.
International Copyright Secured   All Rights Reserved

There's a Small Hotel

from ON YOUR TOES

Words by LORENZ HART
Music by RICHARD RODGERS

Copyright © 1936 by Chappell & Co.
Copyright Renewed
The interest of Richard Rodgers for the extended term of copyright assigned to the Rodgers Family Partnership (Administered by Williamson Music)
Rights on behalf of The Estate of Lorenz Hart administered by WB Music Corp.
International Copyright Secured   All Rights Reserved

Where or When

from BABES IN ARMS

Words by LORENZ HART
Music by RICHARD RODGERS

With tender expression

It seems we stood and talked like this be-fore. We looked at each oth-er in the same way then, But I can't re-mem-ber where or when. The clothes you're wear-ing are the

Copyright © 1937 by Chappell & Co.
Copyright Renewed
The interest of Richard Rodgers for the extended term of copyright assigned to the Rodgers Family Partnership (Administered by Williamson Music)
Rights on behalf of The Estate of Lorenz Hart administered by WB Music Corp.
International Copyright Secured   All Rights Reserved

clothes you wore. The smile you are smil- ing you were

smil- ing then, But I can't re- mem- ber where or

when. Some things that

hap- pen for the first time,

Seem to be hap- pen- ing a- gain.

September Song
from KNICKERBOCKER HOLIDAY

Words by MAXWELL ANDERSON
Music by KURT WEILL

Copyright © 1938 by DeSylva, Brown & Henderson, Inc.
Copyright Renewed, Chappell & Co. and TRO-Hampshire House Publishing Corp. owners of publication and allied rights
International Copyright Secured   All Rights Reserved

Well, Did You Evah?

from DUBARRY WAS A LADY

Words and Music by
COLE PORTER

Moderato (brightly)

He: When you're out in smart so - ci - e - ty And you sud-den-ly get bad news, You mus - n't show an - xi - e - ty, She: And pro - ceed to sing the blues. He: For ex - am-ple, tell me some-thing bad, Some-thing

Copyright © 1940, 1946 by Chappell & Co.
Copyrights Renewed, Assigned to John F. Wharton, Trustee of the Cole Porter Musical and Literary Property Trusts
Chappell & Co. owner of publication and allied rights throughout the world
International Copyright Secured   All Rights Reserved

Bewitched
from PAL JOEY

Words by LORENZ HART
Music by RICHARD RODGERS

VERA:

He's a fool and don't I know it. But a fool can have his charms.

I'm in love and don't I show it, Like a babe in arms. Love's the same old

sad sen-sa-tion. Late-ly I've not slept a wink Since this half-pint im-i-ta-tion

Copyright © 1941 by Chappell & Co.
Copyright Renewed
International Copyright Secured   All Rights Reserved

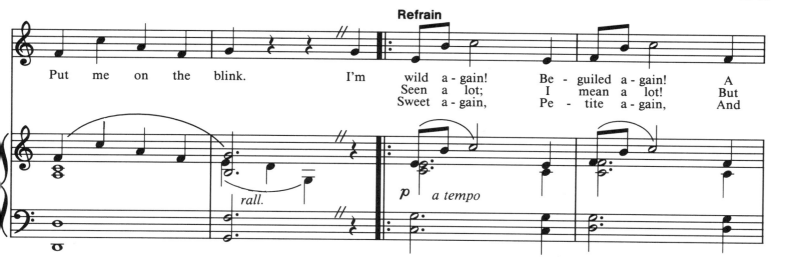

Refrain

Put me on the blink. I'm

wild a - gain!   Be - guiled a - gain!   A
Seen a lot;   I mean a lot!   But
Sweet a - gain,   Pe - tite a - gain,   And

rall.   *p*   *a tempo*

simp-er - ing, whimp-er - ing child a - gain.   Be - witched,   both-ered and be - wil - dered am
now I'm like sweet sev - en - teen a lot.   Be - witched,   both-ered and be - wil - dered am
on my pro - verb - i - al seat a - gain.   Be - witched,   both-ered and be - wil - dered am

f   *p*

I._____
I._____
I._____

   I'll   Could-n't sleep   And would-n't sleep   Un -
sing to him   Each spring to him   And
What am I?   Half shot am I.   To

3   3

p

til I could sleep where I should-n't sleep. Be - witched, both-ered and be - wil - dered am
wor - ship the trou-sers that cling to him. Be - witched, both-ered and be - wil - dered am
think that he loves me, So hot am I. Be - witched, both-ered and be - wil - dered am

I.
I.
I.

Lost my heart, but what of it?
When he talks He is seek - ing
Though at first we said "No, sir."

My mis - take, I a - gree.
Words to get off his chest.
Now we're two lit- tle dears.

He's a laugh, but I love it____ Be - cause the
Hor - i - zon - tal - ly speak - ing,__ He's at his
You might say we are clos - er____ Than Roe - buck

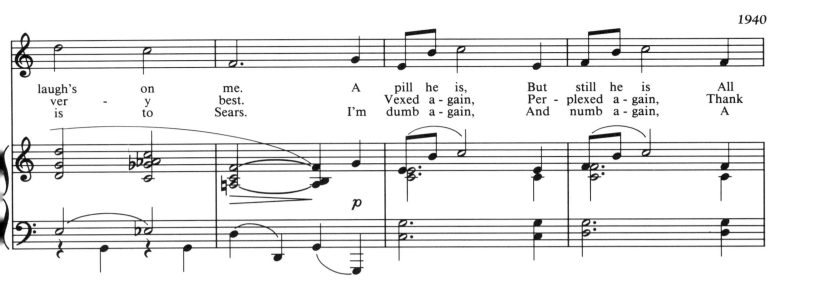

laugh's on me. A pill he is, But still he is, All
ver - y best. Vexed a - gain, Per - plexed a - gain, Thank
is - to Sears. I'm dumb a - gain, And numb a - gain, A

p

wine and I'll keep him un - til he is Be - witched, both - ered and be - wil - dered like
God I can be o - ver - sexed a - gain. Be - witched, both - ered and be - wil - dered am
rich, read - y, ripe lit - tle plum a - gain. Be - witched, both - ered and be - wil - dered am

f *p*

1,2 3

me. _____
I. _____ I. _____

mf *mf* *rall.*

8va

The Saga of Jenny

from LADY IN THE DARK

Words by IRA GERSHWIN
Music by KURT WEILL

TRO - © Copyright 1941 (Renewed) Hampshire House Publishing Corp., New York, New York, and Chappell & Co.
International Copyright Secured
All Rights Reserved Including Public Performance For Profit
Used by Permission

Refrain Cm (leisurely)

1. Jen-ny made her mind up when she was three, She, her-self, was going to trim the
2. Jen-ny made her mind up when she was twelve, That in-to for-eign lan-guag-es
3. Jen-ny made her mind up at twen-ty-two, To get her-self a hus-band was the
4. Jen-ny made her mind up at thir-ty-nine,— She would take a trip to the
5. Jen-ny made her mind up at fif-ty-one,— She would write her mem-moirs be-

Christ - mas   tree;— Christ - mas Eve she lit the can - dles, tossed the
she   would delve,— But   at   sev - en - teen to Vas - sar   it   was
thing   to   do, —   She   got her - self all dolled up   in   her
Ar   -   gen - tine.— She   was   on - ly on va - ca - tion, but the
fore she was   done,— The   ver - y day her book was pub - lished

ta-pers a - way. Lit - tle Jen - ny was an or - phan   on   Christ - mas day.—
quite   a blow That in twen-ty sev - en lan-guag-es   she   could-n't say no.—
sat-ins and furs, And she got her-self a hus-band,   but   he was-n't hers..
Lat-ins a - gree, Jen - ny was the one who start - ed the Good Neigh-bor Pol - i - cy.
his-t'ry re - lates There were wives who shot their hus-bands in some thir-ty-three states.

(small notes only for 4th refrain)

6. Jen - ny made her mind up at sev - en - ty - five, —

She would live to be the old - est wom - an a - live, — But

gin and rum and des - ti - ny play fun - ny tricks — And poor

Jen - ny kicked the buck - et at sev - en - ty - six. —

An - y - one with vi - sion, Comes to this de - ci - sion, Don't make up, you should - n't make up, You

must - n't make up, oh nev - er make up An - y - one with vi - sion, Comes to this de - ci - sion,

Don't — make — up — your — mind! _____

Nobody's Heart

from BY JUPITER

Words by LORENZ HART
Music by RICHARD RODGERS

Copyright © 1942 by Chappell & Co.
Copyright Renewed
International Copyright Secured   All Rights Reserved

1943

Oh, What a Beautiful Mornin'
from OKLAHOMA!

Lyrics by OSCAR HAMMERSTEIN II
Music by RICHARD RODGERS

Copyright © 1943 by WILLIAMSON MUSIC
Copyright Renewed
International Copyright Secured   All Rights Reserved

Lonely Town

from ON THE TOWN

Words by BETTY COMDEN and ADOLPH GREEN
Music by LEONARD BERNSTEIN

Ga-bey's com-in', Ga-bey's com-in' to town,___ So what? Who cares? Back on the ship it seemed such a snap: You'd tap a girl on the shoul-der,

© 1945 WARNER BROS. INC. (Renewed)
All Rights Reserved

If I Loved You

from CAROUSEL

Lyrics by OSCAR HAMMERSTEIN II
Music by RICHARD RODGERS

Copyright © 1945 by WILLIAMSON MUSIC
Copyright Renewed
International Copyright Secured   All Rights Reserved

I Got the Sun in the Morning

from ANNIE GET YOUR GUN

Words and Music by
IRVING BERLIN

© Copyright 1946 by Irving Berlin
Copyright Renewed
International Copyright Secured   All Rights Reserved

Check-ing up____ on what I have __ and what I have - n't, ____

what do I find? __ A health - y bal - lance on the cred - it side.__

Got no dia - mond,

got no pearl,__ still I think __ I'm a luck - y girl.__ I got the

How Are Things in Glocca Morra
from FINIAN'S RAINBOW

Words by E.Y. HARBURG
Music by BURTON LANE

Copyright © 1946 by Chappell & Co.
Copyright Renewed
International Copyright Secured   All Rights Reserved

Brush Up Your Shakespeare

from KISS ME, KATE

Words and Music by
COLE PORTER

Copyright © 1949 by Cole Porter
Copyright Renewed, Assigned to John F. Wharton, Trustee of the Cole Porter Musical and Literary Property Trusts
Chappell & Co. owner of publication and allied rights throughout the world
International Copyright Secured   All Rights Reserved

rav - in' _____ Is the po - et peo - ple call _____

The bard of Strat - ford - on - A - von.

Refrain

Brush up your Shake - speare, Start
Brush up your Shake - speare, Start
Brush up your Shake - speare, Start

quot - ing him now _____ Brush up your
quot - ing him now _____ Brush up your
quot - ing him now _____ Brush up your

* *Cockney for take*

Some Enchanted Evening
from SOUTH PACIFIC

Lyrics by OSCAR HAMMERSTEIN II
Music by RICHARD RODGERS

Some en-chant-ed eve-ning
Some en-chant-ed eve-ning

You may see a stran-ger,
Some-one may be laugh-ing,

You may see a stran-ger
You may hear her laugh-ing

A-cross a
A-cross a

crowd-ed room
crowd-ed room

And some-how you know,
And night af-ter night.

Copyright © 1949 by Richard Rodgers and Oscar Hammerstein II
Copyright Renewed
WILLIAMSON MUSIC owner of publication and allied rights throughout the world
International Copyright Secured   All Rights Reserved

Luck Be a Lady

from GUYS AND DOLLS

By FRANK LOESSER

© 1950 (Renewed) FRANK MUSIC CORP.
All Rights Reserved

La - dy with me.

A la - dy does - n't leave her es - cort It is - n't

fair It is - n't nice! A

la - dy does - n't wan - der all ov - er the room and

blow on some oth - er guy's dice. So,

Hello, Young Lovers

from THE KING AND I

Lyrics by OSCAR HAMMERSTEIN II
Music by RICHARD RODGERS

Copyright © 1951 by Richard Rodgers and Oscar Hammerstein II
Copyright Renewed
WILLIAMSON MUSIC owner of publication and allied rights throughout the world
International Copyright Secured   All Rights Reserved

Wish You Were Here

from WISH YOU WERE HERE

Words and Music by
HAROLD ROME

Copyright © 1952 by Harold Rome
Copyright Renewed, Assigned to Chappell & Co.
International Copyright Secured   All Rights Reserved

Stranger in Paradise
from KISMET

Words and Music by ROBERT WRIGHT
and GEORGE FORREST
(Music Based on Themes of A. BORODIN)

Copyright © 1953 Frank Music Corp.
Copyright renewed and assigned to Scheffel Music Corp., New York, NY
All rights controlled by Scheffel Music Corp.
All Rights Reserved   International Copyright Secured

A Sleepin' Bee

from HOUSE OF FLOWERS

Lyric by TRUMAN CAPOTE and HAROLD ARLEN
Music by HAROLD ARLEN

© 1954 (Renewed) HAROLD ARLEN and TRUMAN CAPOTE
All Rights Controlled by HARWIN MUSIC CO.
All Rights Reserved

1954

All of You
from SILK STOCKINGS

Words and Music by
COLE PORTER

Fox Trot Tempo

mf

With bounce, not too fast

mp

After watch-ing her ap-peal from ev-'ry an-gle,

There's a big ro-man-tic deal I've got to wan-gle.

For I've fall-en for a

Copyright © 1954 by Cole Porter
Copyright Renewed, Assigned to Robert H. Montgomery, Trustee of the Cole Porter Musical and Literary Property Trusts
Chappell & Co. owner of publication and allied rights throughout the world
International Copyright Secured   All Rights Reserved

I've Grown Accustomed to Her Face

from MY FAIR LADY

Words by ALAN JAY LERNER
Music by FREDERICK LOEWE

Copyright © 1956 by Alan Jay Lerner and Frederick Loewe
Copyright Renewed
Chappell & Co. owner of publication and allied rights throughout the world
International Copyright Secured   All Rights Reserved

1956

238

Till There Was You

from Meredith Willson's THE MUSIC MAN

By MEREDITH WILLSON

© 1950, 1957 (Renewed) FRANK MUSIC CORP. and MEREDITH WILLSON MUSIC
All Rights Reserved

You Are Beautiful

from FLOWER DRUM SONG

Lyrics by OSCAR HAMMERSTEIN II
Music by RICHARD RODGERS

Copyright © 1958 by Richard Rodgers and Oscar Hammerstein II
Copyright Renewed
WILLIAMSON MUSIC owner of publication and allied rights throughout the world
International Copyright Secured   All Rights Reserved

Everything's Coming Up Roses

from GYPSY

Words by STEPHEN SONDHEIM
Music by JULE STYNE

Copyright © 1959 by Norbeth Productions, Inc. and Stephen Sondheim
Copyright Renewed
All Rights Administered by Chappell & Co.
International Copyright Secured   All Rights Reserved

Camelot
from CAMELOT

Words by ALAN JAY LERNER
Music by FREDERICK LOEWE

Copyright © 1960, 1961 by Alan Jay Lerner and Frederick Loewe
Copyright Renewed
Chappell & Co. owner of publication and allied rights throughout the world
International Copyright Secured   All Rights Reserved

1960

252

I Believe in You

from HOW TO SUCCEED IN BUSINESS WITHOUT REALLY TRYING

By FRANK LOESSER

© 1961 (Renewed) FRANK MUSIC CORP.
All Rights Reserved

1961

cool clear eyes of a seek-er of wis-dom and truth,

Yet there's that slam bang tang rem - i - nis-cent of gin and ver -

mouth. Oh I Be - lieve In You,____

____ I Be - lieve In You.____

R.H.

256

Comedy Tonight

from A FUNNY THING HAPPENED ON THE WAY TO THE FORUM

Words and Music by
STEPHEN SONDHEIM

Some-thing fa-mil - iar, some-thing pe - cul - iar,
Some-thing con-vul - sive, some-thing re - pul - sive,

Some-thing for ev-'ry-one, a Com-e-dy To - night!
Some-thing for ev-'ry-one, a Com-e-dy To - night!

Some-thing ap-peal - ing, some-thing ap - pal - ling,
Some-thing es-thet - ic, some-thing fre - net - ic,

Copyright © 1962 by Stephen Sondheim
Copyright Renewed
Burthen Music Co., Inc., owner of publication and allied rights throughout the world
Chappell & Co., sole selling agent
International Copyright Secured   All Rights Reserved

Where Is Love?

from The Columbia Pictures-Romulus Film OLIVER!

Words and Music by
LIONEL BART

Slowly, but rhythmically

Where _____ Is Love? Does it fall from skies a - bove?

Is it un - der - neath the wil - low tree _ that I've been dream - ing of?

Where _____ is she who I close my eyes to see? Will I ev - er know the

© Copyright 1960 (Renewed) Lakeview Music Co. Ltd., London, England
TRO - Hollis Music, Inc., New York, controls all publication rights for the U.S.A. and Canada
International Copyright Secured
All Rights Reserved Including Public Performance For Profit
Used by Permission

Hello, Dolly!

from HELLO, DOLLY!

Music and Lyric by
JERRY HERMAN

© 1963 (Renewed) JERRY HERMAN
All Rights Controlled by EDWIN H. MORRIS & COMPANY, A Division of MPL Communications, Inc.
All Rights Reserved

Cabaret
from CABARET

Music by JOHN KANDER
Words by FRED EBB

Lyrics:

What good is sit-ting a-lone in your room?_
Put down the knit-ting, the book and the broom,_

Come hear the mu-sic play;_____
Time for a hol-i-day;_____

Life is a cab-a-ret, old chum,_ Come to the

Copyright © 1966 by Alley Music Corporation and Trio Music Company, Inc.
All Rights Administered by Hudson Bay Music, Inc.
International Copyright Secured   All Rights Reserved
Used by Permission

1967

Maman
from MATA HARI

Lyric by MARTIN CHARNIN
Music by EDWARD THOMAS

© 1967, 1968 MARTIN CHARNIN and EDWARD THOMAS
All Rights Throughout the World Controlled by MPL Communications, Inc.
All Rights Reserved

Promises, Promises
from PROMISES, PROMISES

Lyric by HAL DAVID
Music by BURT BACHARACH

With fire

CHUCK:

Prom - is - es, prom - is - es, I'm all through with prom - is - es, prom - is - es now. I don't know how I got the nerve to walk out. If I shout, Re -

Copyright © 1968 Blue Seas Music, Inc. and Jac Music Co.
International Copyright Secured   All Rights Reserved

end. I won't pre - tend That what was wrong can be right. Ev - 'ry night I'll sleep now; No more lies. Things that I prom - ised my - self fell a - part,

But I found my heart.

Prom - is - es, their kind of prom - is - es can just de - stroy your life.

Oh, prom - is - es, those kind of prom - is - es take all the joy from

life. Oh, prom - is - es, prom - is - es,

cresc.

Somebody

from CELEBRATION

Words by TOM JONES
Music by HARVEY SCHMIDT

Copyright © 1969 by Tom Jones and Harvey Schmidt
All Rights Administered by Chappell & Co.
International Copyright Secured   All Rights Reserved

1969

283

Being Alive

from COMPANY

Words and Music by
STEPHEN SONDHEIM

Copyright © 1970 by Range Road Music Inc., Quartet Music Inc. and Rilting Music, Inc.
All Rights Administered by Herald Square Music, Inc.
International Copyright Secured   All Rights Reserved
Used by Permission

Broadway Baby
from FOLLIES

Words and Music by
STEPHEN SONDHEIM

Copyright © 1971 by Range Road Music Inc., Quartet Music Inc., Rilting Music, Inc. and Burthen Music Co., Inc.
All Rights Administered by Herald Square Music, Inc.
International Copyright Secured   All Rights Reserved
Used by Permission

Summer Nights
from GREASE

Lyric and Music by WARREN CASEY
and JIM JACOBS

Moderately

Boy: "Sum-mer lov-in', had me a blast."
"She swam by me; she got a cramp."
"Took her bowl-ing in the ar-cade."

Girl: "Sum-mer lov-in' hap-pened so fast."
"He ran by me; got my suit damp."
"We went stroll-ing; drank lem-on-ade."

Boy: "Met a girl, cra-zy for me."
"Saved her life; she near-ly drowned."
"We made out un-der the dock."

Girl: "Met a boy, cute as can be."
"He showed off, splash-ing a-round."
"We stayed out till ten o-clock."

Sum-mer days drift-ing a-way to, uh, oh, those Sum-mer Nights. Well-a, well-a, well-a
Sum-mer sun, some-thing's be-gun. But, uh, oh, those Sum-mer Nights.
Sum-mer fling don't mean a thing. But,

Tacet

© 1972 WARREN CASEY and JIM JACOBS
All Rights Controlled by EDWIN H. MORRIS & COMPANY, A Division of MPL Communications, Inc.
All Rights Reserved

Send in the Clowns
from A LITTLE NIGHT MUSIC

Music and Lyrics by
STEPHEN SONDHEIM

© 1973 REVELATION MUSIC PUBLISHING CORP. and RILTING MUSIC, INC.
International Copyright Secured   All Rights Reserved
A Tommy Valando Publication

I Won't Send Roses

from MACK AND MABEL

Music and Lyric by
JERRY HERMAN

Moderately

mf

I won't send ros - es or hold the door;
fran - tic, my tem - per's cross;

I won't re - mem - ber which dress you wore.
With words ro - man - tic I'm at a loss.

My heart is too much in con - trol, the lack of
I'd be the first one to a - gree that I'm pre -

© 1974 JERRY HERMAN
All Rights Controlled by JERRYCO MUSIC CO.
Exclusive Agent: EDWIN H. MORRIS & COMPANY, A Division of MPL Communications, Inc.
All Rights Reserved

love you, you would be   the last to   know. _____
there's a fight - ing chance   just turn and   go. _____

I won't send ros - es   And ros - es

suit   you   so.   My pace is

suit   you   so. _____

rall.   L. H.

What I Did For Love

from A CHORUS LINE

Music by MARVIN HAMLISCH
Lyric by EDWARD KLEBAN

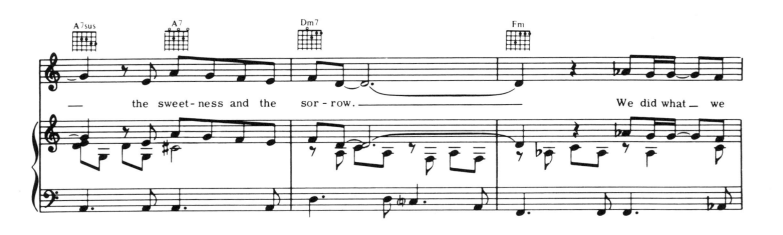

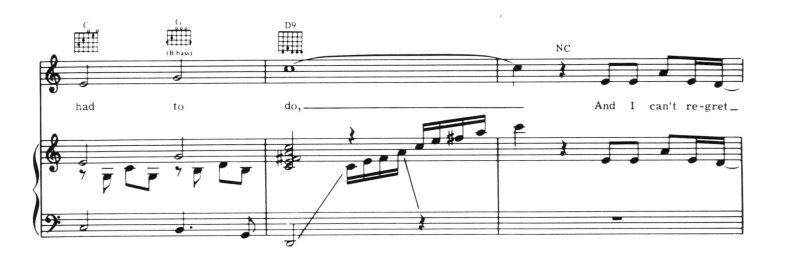

© 1975 MARVIN HAMLISCH and EDWARD KLEBAN
All Rights Controlled by WREN MUSIC CO. and AMERICAN COMPASS MUSIC CORP.
All Rights Reserved

Pretty Lady
from PACIFIC OVERTURES

Words and Music by
STEPHEN SONDHEIM

© 1975 REVELATION MUSIC PUBLISHING CORP. and RILTING MUSIC, INC.
International Copyright Secured   All Rights Reserved
A Tommy Valando Publication

Ad lib
(III:) Pret - ty la - dy, look, I'm on my knees._____ Pret - ty

(I:) Pret - ty la - dy, look, I'm on my knees._____ Pret - ty

(II:) Pret - ty la - dy, look, I'm on my knees. Pret - ty

A tempo
please._____
(I & II:)
please._____

SAILOR II:
Pret - ty la - dy in the pret - ty gar - den, won't-cher stay?_____

simile

Don't go a - way.

I sailed the world for you.

It's the Hard-Knock Life

from ANNIE

Lyric by MARTIN CHARNIN
Music by CHARLES STROUSE

Moderately with a tough edge

It's the hard-knock life for us! It's the hard-knock life for us!

'Stead-a treat-ed ___ we get tricked, 'Stead-a kiss-es ___ we get kicked,

It's the hard-knock ___ life! Got no folks to speak of, so, ___

© 1977 EDWIN H. MORRIS & COMPANY, A Division of MPL Communications, Inc. and CHARLES STROUSE
All Rights Reserved

The Joint is Jumpin'
from AIN'T MISBEHAVIN'

Words by ANDY RAZAF and J.C. JOHNSON
Music by THOMAS "FATS" WALLER

Tempo di-sturb de neighbors

They have a new ex - pres - sion a - long old Har - lem way____ that tells you when a par - ty is ten times more____ than gay.____ To say that things are jump - in' leaves not a sin - gle doubt____ that

Copyright © 1938 (Renewed 1965) RAZAF MUSIC CO., RECORD MUSIC PUBLISHING CO.,
CHAPPELL & CO. and EDWIN H. MORRIS & COMPANY, A Division of MPL Communications, Inc.
Pursuant to Sections 304(c) and 401(b) of the U.S. Copyright Law.
International Copyright Secured   All Rights Reserved

Don't Cry For Me Argentina

from EVITA

Lyric by TIM RICE
Music by ANDREW LLOYD WEBBER

© Copyright 1976, 1977, 1985 by EVITA MUSIC LTD., London, England
Sole Selling Agent MCA MUSIC PUBLISHING, A Division of MCA INC., 1755 Broadway, New York, NY 10019 for the Entire Western Hemisphere
International Copyright Secured   All Rights Reserved

MCA music publishing

all you have to do is look at me to know that ev-'ry word is true.

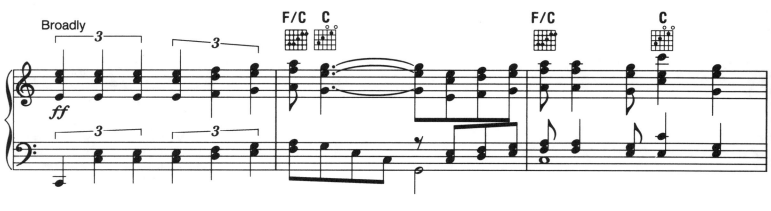

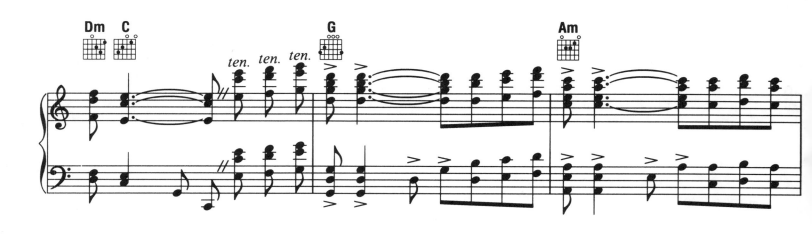

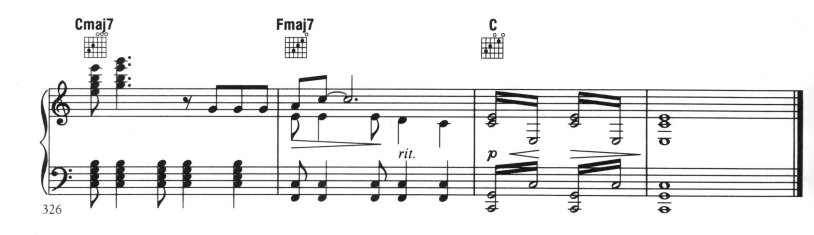

Lullaby of Broadway

from 42ND STREET

Words by AL DUBIN
Music by HARRY WARREN

Moderately fast

© 1935 WARNER BROS. INC. (Renewed)
All Rights Reserved

And I Am Telling You I'm Not Going

from DREAMGIRLS

Lyric by TOM EYEN
Music by HENRY KRIEGER

© 1981 DREAMGIRLS MUSIC, DREAMETTES MUSIC, TOM EYEN and MIROKU MUSIC, LTD.
All rights administered jointly by WB MUSIC CORP. and WARNER-TAMERLANE PUBLISHING CORP.
All Rights Reserved

Memory
from CATS

Music by ANDREW LLOYD WEBBER
Lyrics by TREVOR NUNN and T.S. ELIOT

Mid - night.___ Not a sound from the pave - ment.___ Has the moon lost her mem - 'ry?___ She is smil - ing a - lone.___ In the lamp - light the wi - thered leaves col - lect at my feet___ And the wind___ be - gins to moan.

Mem - 'ry.___ All a-lone in the moon - light___ I can smile at the old days,___ I was beau - ti - ful

Copyright © 1981 The Really Useful Group Ltd. and Faber and Faber Ltd.
All Rights for The Really Useful Group Ltd. for the United States and Canada Administered by Songs Of PolyGram International, Inc.
International Copyright Secured   All Rights Reserved

The Best of Times
from LA CAGE AUX FOLLES

Music and Lyric by
JERRY HERMAN

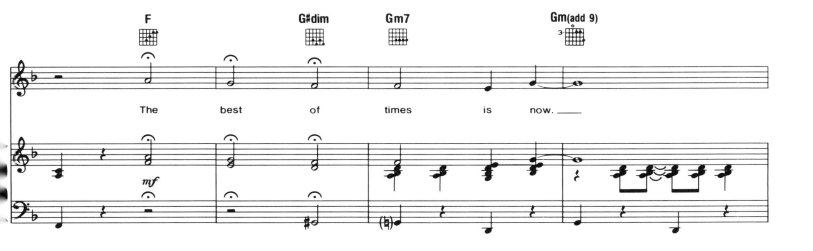

The best of times is now. _____

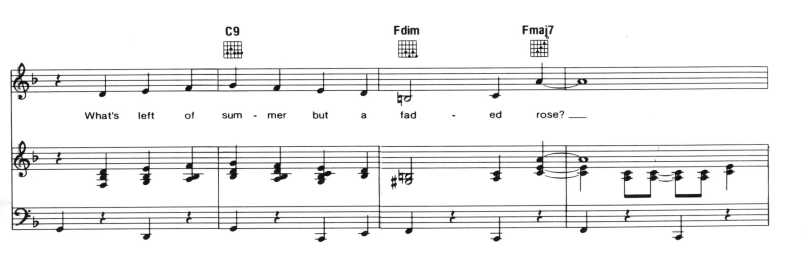

What's left of sum- mer but a fad - ed rose? _____

© 1983 JERRY HERMAN
All Rights Controlled by JERRYCO MUSIC CO.
Exclusive Agent: EDWIN H. MORRIS & COMPANY, A Division of MPL Communications, Inc.
All Rights Reserved

And make this mo - ment last _____

be - cause the best of times is now, is now, is

now. The best of

times is now. _____ What's left of sum - mer but a

Slower

Sunday

from SUNDAY IN THE PARK WITH GEORGE

Words and Music by
STEPHEN SONDHEIM

© 1984 REVELATION MUSIC PUBLISHING CORP. and RILTING MUSIC, INC.
International Copyright Secured   All Rights Reserved
A Tommy Valando Publication

through our per-fect park, Paus-ing on a

cresc. poco a poco

Sun-day _____ by the cool ___ blue tri-an-gu-lar wa-ter _____

cresc. poco a poco

___ on the soft ___ green el-lip-ti-cal grass As we pass

f

dim.

through ar-range-ments of sha-dows ___ towards the ver-ti-cals of

dim.

1984

354

Unexpected Song
from SONG & DANCE

Music by ANDREW LLOYD WEBBER
Lyrics by DON BLACK

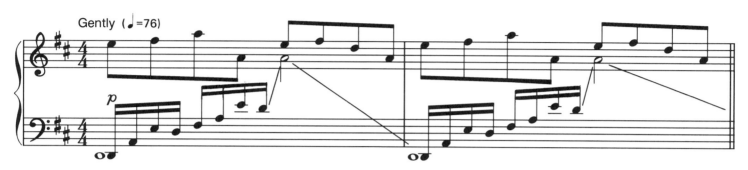

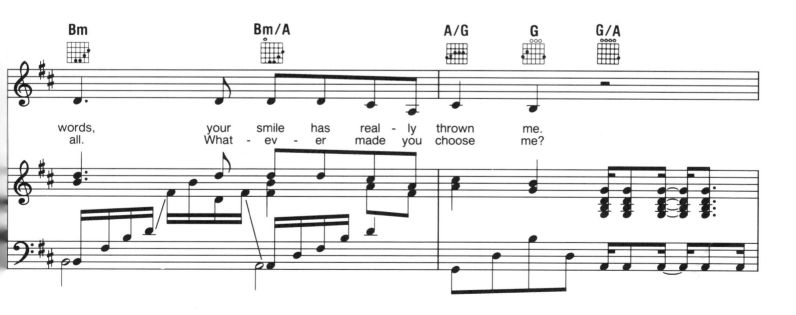

Copyright © 1982 The Really Useful Group Ltd. and Steam Power Music Ltd.
All Rights for the United States and Canada Administered by PolyGram International Publishing, Inc. and Songs Of PolyGram International, Inc.
International Copyright Secured   All Rights Reserved

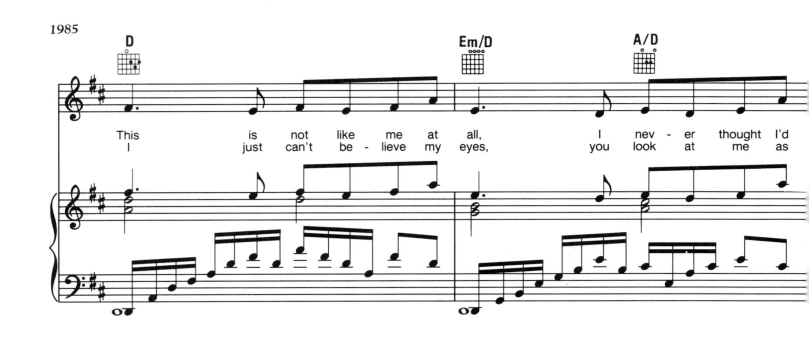

This is not like me at all, I nev - er thought I'd
I just can't be - lieve my eyes, you look at me as

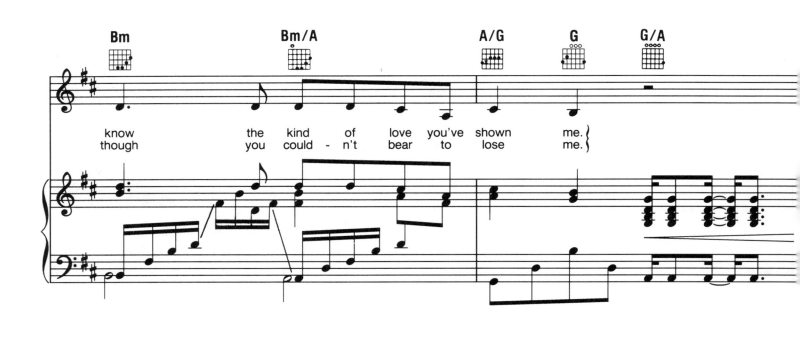

know the kind of love you've shown me.
though you could - n't bear to lose me.

Now no mat - ter where I am, no mat - ter what I do, I see your face ap

song, an un-ex-pect-ed song that on-ly we are hear - ing.

Like an un-ex-pect-ed song, an un-ex-pect-ed song that on-ly we are

hear - ing.

Leaning on a Lamp-Post

from ME AND MY GIRL

Words and Music by
NOEL GAY

Copyright © 1937 Richard Armitage Ltd.
Copyright Renewed
All Rights Managed in the U.S. by PolyGram International Publishing, Inc.
International Copyright Secured   All Rights Reserved

Bring Him Home
from LES MISÉRABLES

Music by CLAUDE-MICHEL SCHÖNBERG
Lyrics by HERBERT KRETZMER and ALAIN BOUBLIL

Andante

L.H. over R.H.

VALJEAN:

God on high, _____ hear my prayer. _____

In my need _____ You have al-ways been there. _____

He is young, _____ he's a-fraid. _____ Let him

Music and Lyrics Copyright © 1986 by Alain Boublil Music Ltd. (ASCAP)
Mechanical and Publication Rights for the USA Administered by Alain Boublil Music Ltd. (ASCAP)
c/o Stephen Tenenbaum & Co., Inc., 605 Third Ave., New York, NY 10158 Tel. (212) 922-0625, Fax (212) 922-0626
International Copyright Secured. All Rights Reserved. This music is copyright. Photocopying is illegal.
All Performance Rights Restricted.

rest heaven blessed. Bring him
poco più mosso
home, bring him home,
rall.
bring him
più mosso
home. He's like the son I might have known if God had grant-ed me a
mf
son. The sum-mers die one by one. How soon they fly on and

The Music of the Night
from THE PHANTOM OF THE OPERA

Music by ANDREW LLOYD WEBBER
Lyrics by CHARLES HART and RICHARD STILGOE

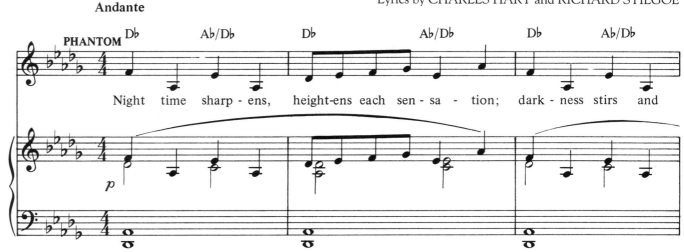

Night time sharp-ens, height-ens each sen-sa-tion; dark-ness stirs and

wakes im-ag-in-a-tion. Si-lent-ly the sen-ses a-ban-don their de-fen-ces.

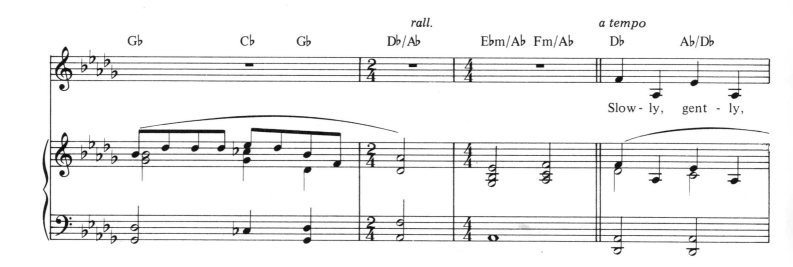

Slow-ly, gent-ly,

Copyright © 1986 The Really Useful Group Ltd.
All Rights for the United States and Canada Administered by PolyGram International Publishing, Inc.
International Copyright Secured   All Rights Reserved

Bonjour Amour

from GRAND HOTEL

Words and Music by
MAURY YESTON

With energy ♩.= 104

Copyright © 1989 by Yeston Music, Ltd.
Worldwide rights administered by Cherry River Music (BMI)
International Copyright Secured   All Rights Reserved

Love Changes Everything

from ASPECTS OF LOVE

Music by ANDREW LLOYD WEBBER
Lyrics by DON BLACK and CHARLES HART

© Copyright 1988 The Really Useful Group Ltd.
All Rights for North America Controlled by R&H Music Co.
International Copyright Secured   All Rights Reserved

Off ____ in - to the world we go, plan-ning fu - tures, shap-ing years.

Love ____ bursts in and sud-den-ly, all our wis-dom dis-ap-pears.

Love ____ makes fools of ev-ery-one: all the rules we make are

Sun and Moon
from MISS SAIGON

Music by CLAUDE-MICHEL SCHÖNBERG
Lyrics by RICHARD MALTBY JR. and ALAIN BOUBLIL
Adapted from original French Lyrics by ALAIN BOUBLIL

KIM: You are ___ sun - light ___ and I ___ moon, ___ joined by ___ the gods of for - tune, ___ mid - night ___ and high noon ___ shar - ing ___ the sky.

Music and Lyrics Copyright © 1987 by Alain Boublil Music Ltd. (ASCAP)
English Lyrics Copyright © 1988 by Alain Boublil Music Ltd. (ASCAP)
Additional Music and English Lyrics Copyright © 1989 and 1991 by Alain Boublil Music Ltd. (ASCAP)
This Arrangement Copyright © 1993 by Alain Boublil Music Ltd. (ASCAP)
Mechanical and Publication Rights for the U.S.A. Administered by Alain Boublil Music Ltd. (ASCAP)
c/o Stephen Tenenbaum & Co., Inc., 605 Third Ave., New York, NY 10158 Tel.(212) 922-0625 Fax (212) 922-0626
International Copyright Secured.   All Rights Reserved.   This music is copyright.   Photocopying is illegal.
All Performance Rights Restricted.

Embraceable You

from CRAZY FOR YOU

Music and Lyrics by GEORGE GERSHWIN
and IRA GERSHWIN

© 1930 WB MUSIC CORP. (Renewed)
All Rights Reserved

The Kiss of the Spider Woman

from KISS OF THE SPIDER WOMAN

Lyrics by FRED EBB
Music by JOHN KANDER

SPIDER WOMAN

Soon - er or la - ter you're cer - tain to meet in the bed - room, the
Soon - er or la - ter your love will ar - rive and he touch - es your

par - lor or e - ven the street. There's no place on earth you're
heart. You're a - lert and a - live and there's on - ly one pin that can

© 1992, 1993 FIDDLEBACK MUSIC PUBLISHING CO., INC. and KANDER & EBB, INC. (BMI)
International Copyright Secured   All Rights Reserved
A Tommy Valando Publication

TO CODA